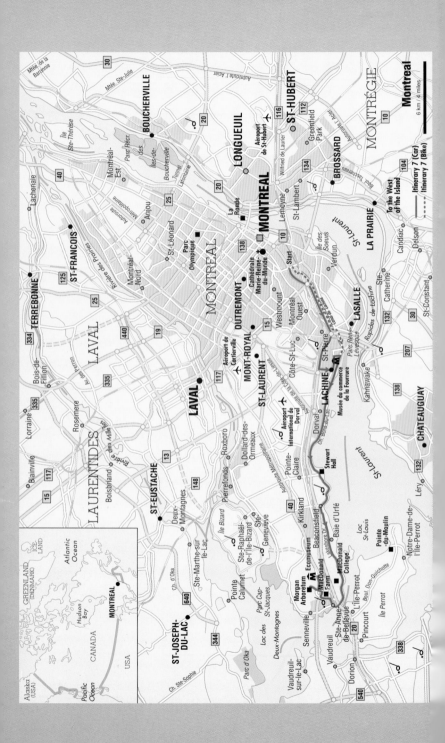

Welcome!

From its beginnings as a frontier outpost of New France, Montréal has become Canada's most sophisticated city, a leap largely propelled by the fur trade. Its modern-day confidence and international image befit its dramatic location, at the confluence of the St Lawrence and Ottawa rivers. Dynamic rather than static, the city flourishes on differences – from extremes in temperature to the French–English language divide.

In these pages *Insight Guides'* correspondent in Montréal, Alice Klement, captures the city's energy, history and style. Her carefully crafted itineraries combine 'must-see attractions' with hidden corners that only someone intimately acquainted with Montréal is likely to know. Three full-day itineraries concentrating on the big museums and monuments are followed by a Pick & Mix section in which she focuses on particular pleasures, from watching Les Canadiens play hockey at the Molson Centre, to joining locals at the casino, or taking a cycle ride along the Canal de Lachine to the western tip of the island. She also shares her knowledge of the city's best restaurants, hotels and shops.

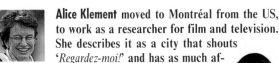

Alice Klement moved to Montréal from the US, to work as a researcher for film and television. She describes it as a city that shouts *'Regardez-moi!'* and has as much affection for it today as when she received her first two-cheek kiss here over two decades ago. Such kisses are just some of the many pleasures she has discovered in the city. In this guide, she says, she has tried to include all Montréal's 'landmarks, treats and oddities.'

C O N T E N T S

Pages 2/3: aerial view of Montréal

Excursion

Pages 8/9: making friends in Le Vieux-Montréal

Shopping, Eating Out & Nightlife

Calendar of Events

Practical Information

Maps

HISTORY & CULTURE

Odd as it may seem, Montréal owes its start to beavers. For two centuries, fur – those who wanted it, those who traded it – propelled the city from frontier outpost to major metropolis. When French explorer Jacques Cartier first came up-river in 1535, he encountered Amerindians in an island village named Hochelaga, 'Place of the Beaver.' Cartier also spotted two

Bataille de Champlain

landmarks – a river and mountain – that even today shape Montréal's destiny and demeanor. He then did what European adventurers out for *le Christ et le Roi* predictably did: he started re-naming. He christened the river St-Lawrence to honor the saint on whose feast day he arrived, and he christened the hill *Le Mont du Roi* (Mount Royal) for his king.

Almost 80 years passed before Cartier's countrymen followed. In 1611, Samuel de Champlain dug in with a struggling garrison at Place Royale, later known as Pointe-à-Callière. In 1642, colonists established Ville-Marie, spurred by France's wealthy and pious *Societé de Notre-Dame de Montréal*. They came to save heathens, but they couldn't resist the money to be made from the beaver. In France, the aristocracy, the military, and even the middle class hankered for fur garments and hats. With graystone warehouses ready, Montréal became the center of the North American fur trade. Here, beginning in 1645, furs from Indians were brokered for goods from France.

Maisonneuve

In 1663, when New France became a crown colony, Montréal began receiving troops, administrators, and civilizing touches. As the island's *seigneurs*, Sulpician priests laid out streets and built the first church. From a seminary on Place d'Armes they still use today, clerics also developed the Catholic faith. Lay devotees, such as Jeanne Mance, built hospitals, schools, and founded religious orders such as *Les Soeurs Grises* (the Gray Nuns). Colonists built fortifications, fended off Indians, and outlasted catastrophes such as flood, fire and disease. *Les filles du roi*, Frenchwomen eager to marry, arrived to bolster spirits and the population. Facing tough winters and unpredictable crops, the settlers struggled, employing a combination of self-reliance and collective help.

New Old World Battles

Strategically set 1,600 km (1,000 miles) inland from the Atlantic Ocean, Montréal became a port of exit for French explorations. In the 1700s, Montréalers – LaSalle, Marquette, Duluth, de la Vendreye, among others – mapped a continent, extending New France's reach from the Gulf of Mexico to the Rockies and beyond. When European powers struggled to control the Americas, Old World battles were fought out in the New. With fur routes the prize, Montréal faced constant harassment from Indians allied with British troops. Only a peace treaty signed with five Iroquois nations in 1701 allowed the city to get on with normal life.

Then, the Seven Years' War again pitted France against England. In 1759, the British defeated the French on the Plains of Abraham outside Quebec City. A year later Montréal surrendered, ending 200 years of French rule. In 1763, France signed over all territory east of the Mississippi river. This 'conquest' marks the moment when French-speaking *Canadiens*, fearful of losing their language and culture, began a fight for identity. Today, the struggle resounds in Quebec's motto: *Je me souviens* (I remember).

Early map of New France

Now the British faced a dilemma: how to handle the unbending French? In a move both benign and practical, they passed the Quebec Act in 1774 to preserve French civil law, language and the Roman Catholic religion. Some blame today's controversial language laws on this early 'francization.' But it may have been a shrewd move, considering rambunctious American colonies to the south eager to free Montréal from British oppression. In 1775, when American revolutionary forces occupied Montréal, they left without success, and without supporters – only to return for another rebuff in 1812. Meanwhile, demobilized soldiers from Scotland and elsewhere rescued the fur trade abandoned by France. Except for winter, when ice blocked the city's port, business flourished. The new entrepreneurs also exploited other natural resources such as grain and lumber and diversified to railways, breweries and shipbuilding.

Two Solitudes Take Root

Trade with Great Britain led to explosive growth in the first half of the 19th century, with the metropolitan population gaining six-fold. Quebec's two sides – the French-speaking francophones and English-speaking anglophones – split along ethnic, commercial and religious lines. The Catholic clergy fostered an idyllic *ancien régime*: pastoral villages, homogeneous neighborhoods, shared traditions, no immigrants. Francophones were urged to turn their backs on commerce as *l'affaire des Anglais*, the business of the English.

At Place d'Armes and Square Dorchester, French Catholic churches faced English banks and offices. In 1817, anglophones founded the Bank of Montréal, Canada's first, to finance such ventures as the Canal de Lachine. Meanwhile francophones built churches, including Basilique Notre-Dame, then the largest church in North America. Within decades, steeples dominated the city's skyline, prompting one American visitor to tag Montréal 'a mountain of churches.'

An idealised image of French Canadian life in the 19th century

Patriotes leader, Louis-Joseph Papineau

Incorporated into Canada in 1832, Montréal prospered as its premier metropolis. It had a great port and grain depot, and was the leading center of banks, railroads, industry and insurance. This buffered the drop in fur shipments, which by 1820 accounted for only 5 percent of city exports. Despite the lost sheen of its coat, the beaver guarded a crest adopted by the city to honor its major ethnic groups: French, English, Scottish and Irish. The beaver also flourished on maps, medals, flags, even on a newspaper masthead. The city endorsed the optimistic motto *concordia salus* – salvation through harmony. With a toast to the British king, Montréal francophones and anglophones formed the fraternal St Jean-Baptiste Society in 1834.

But wrenching divisions surfaced in politics and in the streets, a signal of separatism that Jean-Baptiste Day often symbolizes today. In 1837, French Canadian *patriotes* demanded more voice in United Canada's parliament. Their rebellion failed, but leader Louis-Joseph Papineau became a legend in exile. In 1849, when parliament voted to compensate rebels for property losses, outraged Tories burned the parliament building at Place d'Youville. The colonial capital moved to Ottawa the next year, and a British investigator in Quebec reported 'two nations warring in the bosom of a single state,' perhaps the first official record of tension. Unlike today, anglophones may then have outnumbered francophones. Many anglophones (such as the Irish who built the Canal de Lachine) arrived poor, worked poor, and died poor. A few arrived rich and grew richer. With cash to spare from fur fortunes, some even turned philanthropic. Scotsman, James McGill set aside land and money to fund a university which opened in 1829 and still bears his name.

Maps Redrawn

In 1867, amid rhetoric and hyperbole, four Canadian provinces, including Quebec, formed a confederation. Even Quebecers participated as principal architects, in particular Montréal's Sir Georges-Etienne Cartier. Now it seemed Canada would have 'two great founding nations' – England and France. Instead, lives and livelihoods stayed separate. Business boomed, largely for anglophones. Montréal thrived as a center of industry, finance, and commerce, attracting head offices. New business classes grew powerful enough to re-draw the city's map.

In its early years, Montréal thrived behind fortified walls. The elite – drawn from garrison, seminary, merchant house, or royal bureaucracy – lived *côte à côte* with artisans and day laborers, near taverns and boarding houses. But with enemies vanquished or co-opted, the walls fell and the city expanded. By the 1890s, financiers moved

Snow-shoeing clubs flourished

businesses to the slope of Mount Royal and built homes up the hill. Entrepreneurs who controlled a whopping 70 percent of Canada's wealth made this Square Mile golden. Indeed, during the reign of Queen Victoria, Montréal anglophones built a 'city of merchant princes,' with money and power falling disproportionately to the privileged, often unilingually isolated in downtown boardrooms and Westmount mansions. Even sports clubs for curling or snow shoeing became exclusive.

As undisputed Canadian gateway for capital, immigration and ideas, metropolitan Montréal quadrupled its population between 1850 and 1900. Immigrants arrived by sea and by land. Culturally rich, but materially poor, they transformed the city's streets: Jews from eastern Europe, Chinese, Italians, Greeks and Portuguese provided cheap labor, but created massive assimilation problems. This triggered nationalistic urges and unnerved a powerful Church. The conservative Catholic clergy preached *la revanche des berceaux* (the revenge of the cradle) which encouraged the rural faithful to outbreed newcomers. But when the Depression toppled farms, rural Quebecers flooded Montréal, sharing sweatshops with immigrants. Then conscription efforts in World War I and II galvanized francophones against 'British imperialism.' Populist mayor Camillien Houde's protest in 1940 even landed him in jail – a 26-year political tenure as '*Monsieur Montréal*.'

Bonsecours market in the early 20th century

A Noisy Quiet Revolution

After World War II, major changes engulfed the city, including a rise in *Québécois* nationalism. In 1945 two writers new to Montréal published fiction that defined the struggle. Gabrielle Roy wrote *Bonheur d'occasion* about working-class francophones. In the *Two Solitudes*, Hugh MacLennan exposed the gulf between francophones and anglophones. In the 1950s, francophone entrepreneurs finally challenged notions of passive Quebecers as the least educated and most religious North Americans and by the 1960s, liberal *Québécois* masterminded a Quiet Revolution, calling for francophones to be *mâitres chez nous* (masters in our own house). When the Quebec government took over schools and social roles held by the church for 300 years, the provincial theocracy disintegrated. In revitalized Université de Montréal classrooms and *Quartier Latin* cafés, activists forged *souverainiste* dreams.

The city's geography changed, along with its attitudes: 'depression' projects preserved beauty in a botanical garden and on beloved Mount Royal. The St Lawrence Seaway opened in 1959 and ended Montréal's port monopoly. To recuperate, the city went on a building spree in the 1960s, transforming the downtown with skyscrapers, an underground city, and a metro. To create an international profile, populist mayor Jean Drapeau masterminded a successful

Building the Quebec Bridge

World's Fair in 1967. His second venture, the 1976 Summer Olympics, incurred a billion-dollar debt that still hobbles taxpayers.

Immigration also transformed the city. Canada's liberal laws attracted newcomers. Allophones, who spoke neither French nor English as a first language, made the city multilingual and multicultural. When French-only supporters rioted against Italian residents who supported English schools, the Quiet Revolution became noisy. In 1970, bombings, kidnappings and a murder by the radical *Front de Libération du Québec* (FLQ) triggered martial law, and federal troops appeared on Montréal's streets.

Revolutionary extremism eventually passed, but the seed of separatism had already taken root. Politician René Lévesque preached 'French Canada is a genuine nation' and formed the *Parti Québécois* to agitate for French independence. Voted to power in 1976, the PQ passed legislation making French the province's only official language, despite Canada's nationwide endorsement of two founding nations with two languages and cultures. A year later, *La Charte de la Langue Française* was enacted.

Ancient and modern neighbors

From 1980 on, at various times, in various ways, Quebecers lobbied for sovereignty association, constitutional status as a separate and distinct society, even independence. Voter response, inside and outside the province, was negative. When provincial laws addressed *la survivance* of francophone culture, this 'French Fact' alienated many Montréalers. More than 140,000 anglophones, an estimated third of all immigrants, and some 100 corporate headquarters left the city. *A louer* (for rent) and *à vendre* (for sale) signs proliferated as Montréal lost first-city status to Toronto. But nationalists marched, proclaiming: '*Le Québec aux Québécois.*' (Only in 1993 did the hard-line soften, allowing English to appear on public signs.)

Strife still troubles Montréal today, each incidence of violence provoking comparisons with the ferment of the 1970s.

Despite political uncertainty, Montréal enjoyed its 350th birthday party in 1992. Its streamlined crest blossomed everywhere, even in flower beds outside city hall. Only the beaver was missing. In 1993, after the *Bloc Québécois* became the main opposition party in federal parliament, Quebec *souverainistes* touted separation from Canada. The years leading up to the millennium, though blissfully quiet, were occasionally interrupted by the sound of a stray bomb and mutterings that *Les Expos* may pick up and move to the US. Montréalers digested this news, then turned back to finish their croissants and *café au lait*.

'Québécois' demand independence

Historical Highlights

1000 Amerindians populate the St Lawrence Valley.

1535 French explorer Jacques Cartier is the first European to visit the island's Hochelaga village.

1611 Samuel de Champlain sets up a winter garrison at Place Royale.

1642 Colonists arrive to convert the natives and establish a mission at Ville-Marie.

1644 Jeanne Mance establishes the first Montréal hospital.

1653 Marguerite Bourgeoys opens the first school.

1663 The *Messieurs de Saint-Sulpice* obtain title to Montréal island.

1701 A peace treaty between the French and Iroquois assures the colony's survival.

1716 The town is fortified with walls, demolished in 1820.

1737 Marguerite d' Youville founds *Les Soeurs Grises* (Gray Nuns).

1760 A year after the French lose the battle on the Plains of Abraham in Quebec City, Montréal surrenders to the British.

1763 France signs the Treaty of Paris, relinquishing New France to Great Britain.

1774 The Quebec Act is passed to preserve French cultural traditions.

1775 American revolutionary troops enter Montréal.

1778 *Gazette du Commerce et Littéraire*, the city's first newspaper, is published.

1817 The opening of the Bank of Montréal, Canada's first bank.

1821 McGill University receives its Royal Charter.

1824 The Canal de Lachine opens.

1829 Basilique Nôtre-Dame, then the largest church in North America, opens.

1833 The first city council meets and elects a mayor.

1837 *Les Patriotes* rebellion, led by Papineau, is crushed.

1844 Montréal briefly serves as capital of United Canada.

1859 Victoria Bridge spans the St Lawrence river.

1860 Canada's first museum, now Musée des Beaux Arts, opens.

1867 Quebec joins the Dominion of Canada.

1877 Landscape architect FL Olmsted plans Mount Royal Park.

1884 *La Presse*, the city's largest circulation French-language daily newspaper, is founded.

1886 Canada's first transcontinental train leaves from Montréal.

1924 Construction of Oratoire St Joseph begins.

1931 The Botanical Garden opens.

1943 The Université de Montréal is founded.

1954 Jean Drapeau is elected mayor, serving until 1986.

1959 The St Lawrence seaway opens, ending Montréal's port monopoly.

1962 Downtown development begins, with office towers, underground city and metro.

1963 Place-des-Arts opens.

1967 Montréal hosts Expo '67.

1969 The Montréal Expos play their first baseball season.

1970 FLQ terrorist tactics trigger the 'October Crisis.'

1976 Montréal hosts the Summer Olympics.

1990 Mohawks and police confrontation at Oka.

1992 Montréal's 350th birthday.

1994 The *Parti Québécois* win majority in Quebec National Assembly. Premier-elect Jacques Parizeau promises independence referendum.

1995 October 30. Referendum on Quebec sovereignty. 50.6 percent vote No, 49.4 percent vote Yes.

1996 *Parti-Québécois* leader Lucien Bouchard becomes Quebec premier.

1999 Expos baseball club sold to US company.

1999 Former mayor Jean Drapeau dies aged 83.

2001 Summit of American trade talks in Quebec sparks protests.

Montreal City

800 m / 880 yards

•••••• Itinerary B

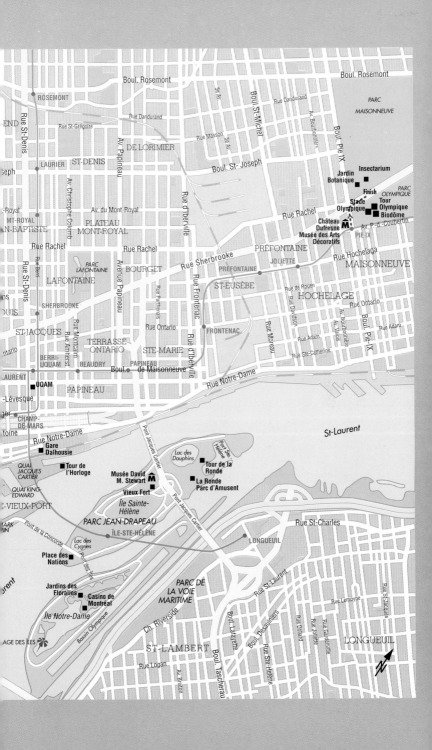

Day Itineraries

Just as Quebec is distinct in Canada, so Montréal is distinct in Quebec. Forget that the city isn't even the capital of its own province, it acts as if it heads a nation. Indeed, as any of its million citizens will boast, Montréal really is *le monde*. This pride is understandable. The city is cosmopolitan, a mix of grand boulevards and twisted alleys, of *avant garde* art and seedy sex shops, of fine wines and beer.

Indeed, it's this blend that gives Montréal its flavor.

The following itineraries will help you discover that. Three day-long tours concentrate on the old city and port, man-made and natural monuments, tempting museums and shops. These are essential viewing – places that reveal the city's heart and history.

Afterwards, choose from a selection of half-day options: absorb St-Laurent's ethnic excitement; frolic on the Expo islands; cheer the Canadiens hockey team; or grab a bike or car, and escape, following a day-long excursion along the Canal de Lachine to charming country-side and towns.

All this is easy to do. To get around, rely on your feet and on Montréal's excellent metro, where many itineraries start and stop. Go slowly, and indulge your curiosity. Don't hesitate to turn a two-hour jaunt into a four-hour stroll. Along the way, sip *café au lait* from a bowl, munch a *baguel*, or chomp *le smoked meat sandwich*. There's something in Montréal to suit every taste.

Stop at a sidewalk café

The Old City and Port

Begin where Montréal did, more than 350 years ago. Be prepared for a full day of walking. See map on page 22.

—To reach the starting point, take the metro to Square Victoria.—

From Square Victoria, walk downhill on Rue McGill, across Rue St-Jacques, and turn left onto Place d'Youville. Head four short blocks to Pointe-à-Callière, the city's first market-place, now a museum. But beware, the pavement is uneven, and horses leave mementos.

All around you is **Le Vieux-Montréal** (the old city): cobblestoned streets wind amid imposing graystones, a touch of New France's *ancien régime*. You will find artists at work, crowded cafés, street entertainers, and so many choices. This area is compact, bounded by St-Jacques to the north, the St-Lawrence river to the south, Berri to the east and McGill to the west – boundaries that match the course of the fortifications in the 1700s.

Pointe-à-Callière, Musée d'Archéologie et d'Histoire de Montréal (Tuesday to Friday

In Le Vieux-Montréal

10am–5pm, Saturday to Sunday 11am–5pm; except July and August 10am–6pm), at 350 Place Royale, occupies the very spot on which Montréal was founded in 1642. This museum of archaeology and history allows you to sift the dirt of six centuries.

At the soaring entrance, Peter Krausz's wall mural *Les Voiles du Temps* (Veils of Time) appropriately parts for you. Take a cozy seat above the ruins, and adjust your bilingual earphones.

Old City crest

Discover Montréal in a 16-minute, multi-media onslaught that explores the city's roots as meeting place and trading center.

Afterwards, descend into the 17th century in a low-lit crypt, and pass over a dried river bed into a maze of foundation walls from the 19th century. Of course, archaeologists got here first, uncovering arrowheads and other objects 1,000 years old. But it's today's technology that dazzles. Virtual figures representing inhabitants of bygone

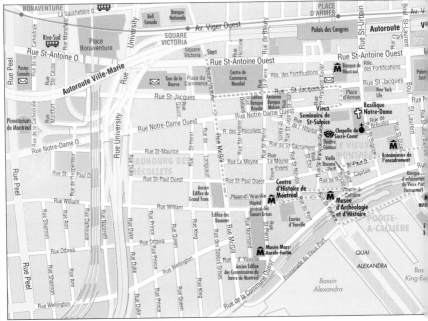

Caryatid carries the weight

eras will tell you about their lives. Before you leave, discover the customs house, now a gift shop, and the restaurant upstairs, for magnificent views.

Outside, across Rue de la Commune, backtrack to 296–316 Place d'Youville to peek into the restored 'stables', former potash sheds far too low for a horse. The attractive inner courtyard, one of Save Montréal's first victories, houses Gibbys (tel: 282-1837), a popular steak house worth considering for dinner. Long ago, residents traveled here by boat on the St-Pierre river. This waterway now flows underground.

If you want more background history, backtrack farther along Rue d'Youville, past the obelisk that honors Mont-réal's 53 founders, to the red bricks and tower of the 'Central Fire Station,' at 335 Place d'Youville. Here, **Le Centre d'histoire de Montréal** (July to September 10am–5pm, closed Monday), offers videos, slides and bilingual audios (but not posted English translations). Twelve rooms on two floors carry you beyond mere dates. Much like *Pointe-à-Callière*, it offers a range of experiences: climbing to Balconville, swaying on a trolley along Ste-Catherine, resting in an easy chair with a radio tuned to programs from 1936, such as *Soirée du Hockey* or *Joyeux Troubadours*. Of special note is ace photographer William Notman's 360° panorama of Montréal photographed in 1889.

Alternatively, continue along Rue de la Commune, named for common pastures that hugged the shoreline in the 18th century. This is **Le Vieux-Port** (Old Port), once the landing for Indians and fur trappers, now a harborfront park stretching 2½ km (1½ miles) and the haunt of cyclists and picnickers. Years ago, when ships moored nearby, wealthy ship owners promenaded here. Follow in their footsteps and enjoy the view: the river and Ile Ste-Hélène, with its redstone Levis tower and huge geodesic dome built for Expo '67. Anticipate crowds here. Not only is this prime tourist territory, locals also gather here on warm weekends.

One of the most exciting additions to the Vieux Port area is the expansion of a former IMAX theater into a fully fledged science museum complex. This new complex, known as iSci – a play on words incorporating both inter-active science, and the French word for 'here' – is located at the foot of the river on **Quay King Edward** (tel: 496-4724 or 1 877-496-4724 toll free). Here, science, natural history and other features play on gigantic screens in surround-sound till late at night – but

'Le Pelican' museum

call ahead to check when less-frequent English screenings are held. There is also a three-hall complex of exhibits geared toward children. In typical Montréal style, both the building and many of the exhibits blur the normally heavy line dividing science and art. The wharf's many other possibilities include Images du Futur, with high-tech

visuals; and a *marché aux puces,* a somewhat tacky flea-market where the odd bargain can usually be found.

Quai Jacques Cartier, situated at the very foot of Boulevard St-Laurent and 6 Rue Berri, is departure point for almost everything that floats: water taxis, a New Orleans paddle boat, flat-bottomed boats, amphibious treks over land and water, jet-boats bound for the Lachine Rapids, shuttles to Parc Jean-Drapeau, romantic cruises. There are plenty of ways to tour the harbor. Don't worry too much about seasickness, as even on windy days the waves are negligible.

If you are not feeling energetic, you could just retire to the riverfront benches and grassy patches to nap, day-dream or people-watch, wander along walkways or bridges through the maze at Bassin de Bonsecours, or perhaps rent a pedal boat and join the ducks. Consider coming back at night, when low lights enhance the romance of the port. At the tip of Quai de l'Horloge stands the **Tour de l'Horloge**, a clock tower honoring sailors lost at sea. Climb up for the panoramic view of La Ronde Ferris wheel tucked under the Pont Jacques Cartier, the clock on top of the Molson headquarters, and old warehouses that once stored furs. To the northeast, the city's modern port still bustles.

Chess mates at the waterfront

To return to town, trek up Rue Bonsecours for half a block. Overlooking the harbor, at 400 St-Paul Est, is the **Chapelle Notre-Dame-de-Bon-Secours** (tel: 282-8670, open May to October, daily 10am–5.30pm; November to April, daily 11am–3.30pm), whose cornerstone was laid in 1657. A statue of the Virgin Mary invites you in. This octagonal building is one of the city's oldest and most charming churches. Note the arched door, wooden belfry and *oeil-de-boeuf* windows in the gable – all traditional *Québécois* touches. The sanctuary is a place of pilgrimage for sailors, who leave model ships suspended from the nave. Look for the oak Madonna that survived three fires and a theft. For a small fee, you can climb another tower (this view is worth it, too) and visit the church's museum. Here is a true treasure house of folklore: 58 miniature dioramas detailing the life of Marguerite Bourgeoys, founder of the religious order Congrégation de Notre-Dame. From the steeple, you can bless ships and crews, as priests used to.

As you exit, turn right for **La Maison du Calvet**, 401 Bonsecours, an 18th-century fieldstone house which is now a café. This was once the home of a French Huguenot merchant jailed for aiding American troops that occupied the city in 1775. Take a *café-et-croissant* break here. Continue southwest along Rue St-Paul, a meandering street laid out in 1672 as the city's main commercial artery. The neo-classical **Marché Bonsecours**, at 330 St-Paul Est, originally housed farmers' stalls, city hall, and even parliament. Now you are likely to find an international art or cultural exhibit here.

In **Rue St-Paul** life spills from restaurants, outdoor cafés, bistros and bars. Its shops attract browsers, though you're more likely to find *camelote* (junk) than quality: too much plastic, too many T-shirts. But there are some exceptions, including **Drags**, 367 St-Paul Est,

Performing tricks on the Place Jacques Cartier

(vintage clothing from the 1940s) and **L'empreinte Cooperative**, 272 St-Paul Est, a cooperative craft shop with a gallery at the back.

Just a few blocks along, **Place Jacques Cartier** bursts upon you. Once the site of a formal garden, this plaza now draws musicians and magicians amid cafés and shops occupying 17th-century houses. As you turn right and climb, look up high for Admiral Horatio Nelson, a tiny figure on top of a very big column. Erected in 1809, long before Nelson became a fixture in London's Trafalgar Square, this is Montréal's oldest monument. Nelson, a Napolean-slayer in a francophone land, faces away from the port, perhaps justifiably nervous in a city of decapitated statues.

At the top of the plaza, look across Rue Notre-Dame for **Hôtel de Ville**, the old city hall, at 275 Notre-Dame Est. Its mansard roof and square-cornered turrets are a tribute to Second Empire style. The balcony has not been used since 1967, when the former French president Charles de Gaulle walked out, shouting the nationalists' cry: '*Vive le Québec libre*' (Long live free Quebec).

Before you head back down the plaza, turn right on Notre-Dame to visit two small museums. The first of these is **Musée du Château Ramezay** (tel: 861-3708, June to September: daily, 10am–6pm; October to May, Tuesday to Sunday, 10am– 4.30pm), at 280 Notre-Dame Est, built in 1705 by the last governor of New France. A plaque

City Hall

Inside Maison du Sir Georges-Etienne Cartier

relates how the building has been home to revolutionary leaders, colonial traders and fur dealers as well as stamp-and-coin fanciers. It now contains portraits.

Rather more interesting is the **Maison du Sir Georges-Etienne Cartier** (January to September: Monday to Friday, 9am–noon and 1–5pm, Saturday and Sunday 10am–6pm; October to December: Wednesday to Sunday only, 10am–noon and 1–5pm), down the block at 458 Notre-Dame Ouest. Upstairs and down, you'll over-hear butlers and chambermaids chatter about the upper class life in the late 19th century. The double house belonged to a promi-nent Quebec statesman. Check out his seven-course dinner menu.

Backtrack now, down the plaza, to the side street **Rue St-Amable**, where artists work and sell their creations. Before heading west on Rue St-Paul, consider **La Marée** (tel: 861-9794) 404 Place St-Jacques, named for the widow of the fur trapper who founded the prestigious Beaver Club. Delicious but pricey seafood dishes are available in a restored 300-year-old stone house filled with tapestry.

Along St-Paul, for another five blocks, eateries abound. Between window-shopping, check out **Steak Frites** (tel: 842-0972) 12 St-Paul Ouest, for an *à volonté* ('all you can eat') meal: steak, salad and real French fries – long, skinny and crisp.

Or turn right, up Rue St-François Xavier, for **Le Bonaparte** (tel: 844-4368), at No 443. It's cozy, with serene lighting and tables raised on little platforms. On the way uphill, check what's playing at **The Centaur** (tel: 288-1229) at No 453, once the city's prosperous stock exchange, now a cornerstone of English theater.

As you re-enter upper town, turn right. Here's **Rue Notre-Dame**, originally known as *Chemin du Roi*, the King's Way, which led to Quebec City; and **Place d'Armes**, where Iroquois and settlers fought, and military men later paraded. The square's central monument, the work of sculptor Philippe Hébert, honors Paul de Chomedey, *Sieur de Maisonneuve* and city founder.

Artists in action on Rue St-Amable

Basilique de Notre-Dame, a Gothic Revival behemoth, at 110 Notre-Dame Ouest, dominates the square. Built in 1829, everything about this church is big: massive twin towers, Temperance and Perseverance (69 m/227 ft); a huge altar surrounded by finely sculpted polychrome wood with gold leaf; even a 12-tonne (13½-ton) bell, *Le Gros Bourdon Jean-Baptiste*, with electronic chimes. Fine acoustics and one of the biggest and most powerful organs on the continent draw music-lovers for Montréal Symphony Orchestra concerts. Reserve seats (tel: 842-3402) for Mozart or Handel in the nave and trace Montréal's history in 12-m (40-ft) stained-glass windows from Limoges.

The **Vieux Séminaire de Saint Sulpice** next door, at 130 Notre-Dame Ouest, may be the city's oldest building. Constructed in 1685, it housed Sulpician landlord-priests who collected rents until seigneurial rights were abolished in 1854. It still houses priests. Look for a wooden clock that's been ticking since 1701, reportedly the oldest outdoor timepiece in North America.

The head office of the **Banque de Montréal**, Canada's first chartered bank, sits opposite, at 119 Rue St-Jacques. The wonderful Roman lobby leads to a free numismatic museum (open during banking hours). Look for marvelous mechanical piggy banks.

In the mid-18th century, Great St-James Street, now **Rue St-Jacques**, rivaled New York City's Wall Street. The street is full of charming details: two especially impressive buildings are the black marble bank lobby of the **Edifice Banque Royale**, at 360 St-Jacques Ouest, and the elegantly restored facade of the **Centre de Commerce Mondial**, the World Trade Center, at 747 Square Victoria. Today's stock exchange, the **Bourse de Montréal**, is nearby on the fourth floor of Place Victoria, 800 Square Victoria.

Back at Place d'Armes, at 511, is the Neo-Roman New York Life building, the city's first modest skyscraper. For an outstanding art deco foyer, head into the Aldred building, next door at 501.

To end the day, try a tour of Old Montréal in a horse-drawn *calèche*, from the cathedral or plaza. There is a set rate, but you can suggest the route. Hop off for dinner at a place you picked earlier. You might also listen for rowdy *chansonniers* at *bôites-à-chanson*, good-natured francophone alternatives to English pubs. One singer usually leads the chorus at **Les Pierrots**, (tel: 861-1270) 104 St-Paul Est, while groups dominate next door at **Deux Pierrots**. A small fee allows you to enter both (8pm–3am, long weekends and summer evenings).

Monumental Montréal

Like other major cities, Montréal is packed with monuments. This cross-city hop takes in the immense Oratoire St-Joseph, the Parc du Mont Royal, the Botanical Gardens and the Parc Olympique, all products of a large vision and ego. See map on page 18–19.

–To reach the start, take the metro to Côte-des-Neiges.–

After a comfortable 10-minute walk south along Chemin de la Côte-des-Neiges and west onto Queen Mary Road, you'll glimpse one of the city's grandest monuments, the **Oratoire St-Joseph** (tel: 733-8211), the city's largest church, nestled at 3800 Queen Mary Road.

If possible, come early. In summer, tour buses jam the parking lots. The main church opens for mass at 6am and closes at 9.30pm. Other areas open later, usually at 9.30am (the basilica closes at 5.15pm and the museum at 5pm). In summer, tours (10am and 2pm) start near the carillons.

This basilica was the big dream of Frère André, the 'Miracle Man of Montréal.' At the beginning of the 20th century, this illiterate caretaker drew followers who believed in his curative powers. By 1924, the Catholic hierarchy had pushed aside its fear of faith healers and approved the construction of a basilica of Canadian granite and reinforced concrete. The Italian Renaissance design was simplified, but the

Oratoire St-Joseph

dome became bigger. At 38 meters (125 ft) in diameter, it is second only to St Peter's in Rome. The construction work took several decades, and Frère André's ability to raise funds was a miracle in itself.

The 283 steps to the church are your first challenge. You might see pilgrims climbing on their knees, reciting a prayer on every step as a sign of devotion. Don't worry, it's okay just to walk up. Getting around the top is easier. At the rear, you'll find an inside walkway ablaze with 3,500 vigil lights, where Canada's patron saint, St Joseph, is honored for many talents, such as terrorising demons, protecting virgins, and curing the sick. The ill and infirm

Window of the Oratoire St-Joseph

who claim to have been cured abandon their crutches and artificial limbs here. Frère André rests in a tomb nearby – at least, most of him does. In a small museum upstairs, look for a case containing his preserved heart, a custom borrowed from Italy and France. It sat in a jar on the main altar until it was stolen in 1973. The outcry was enormous, and relentless, until it was later recovered. So, if you can elbow aside other oglers, take a peek.

Pass quietly to the ornate crypt-church, named for its vault-like architecture. Three escalators lead to a stark chapel in the apse, with bare brick floor, exposed masonry, and folding chairs. From the roof terrace, 152 meters (500 ft) above street level, scan northwest Montréal to Lac St-Louis. Head down and outside if you want to follow the Way of the Cross. But don't toss coins in the fountain – the priests say that's too superstitious. You can listen to noon and mid-afternoon carillon concerts on 56 bells designed for the Eiffel Tower. The ground-level souvenir shop offers ceramic André busts, plus supposedly curative oils taken from the lamps burning in front of St Joseph's statue. Before you leave, look nearby for an unprepossessing wooden chapel. Still standing from 1904, this was the start of the Oratory, now one of the world's largest shrines.

From the Oratory, head to a natural monument, **Parc du Mont-Royal** (daily 6am–midnight). The simplest way to get there is to grab a taxi and enter the park via Remembrance Road or Camillien Houde parkway. Or return to Chemin de la Côte-des-Neiges and take bus 165 or 166 south to the corner of Ridgewood, and transfer to bus 11 east along Côte-des-Neiges and Rue Remembrance. A huge parking lot signals the short walk to man-made **Lac des Castors** (Beaver Lake). If you only want a glimpse of all this, skip the bus transfer, and continue to the Guy-Concordia metro, to cross the city.

Carved from Montréal, Westmount and Outremont, the park covers only 14 percent of the knoll it occupies. Scaled by French

The undulating Parc du Mont-Royal

Mont-Royal cemetery

explorer Jacques Cartier in 1535, the wooded hillside still offers a glimpse of the landscapes enjoyed by Amerindians at the early settlement of Hochelaga. As long ago as 1675, Sulpician landowners laid out farms, orchards and vineyards. Indeed, only recently was the mountain rescued from developers. A handful of wealthy families had shared the property unchallenged until, one cold winter in 1862, a chilly resident clear-cut his property for firewood. Alarmed, the city purchased 182 hectares (450 acres) to save the maples and oaks. In the 1870s, the renowned landscape architect Frederick Law Olmsted, designer of New York City's Central Park, laid a trail to blend nature and city. You can follow this route, somewhat modified, in a 45-minute stroll. The trek is worthwhile, but signs are poor. If you are feeling adventurous, a zigzag trail downhill offers spectacular vistas of mountainside, cemeteries, and towns.

From Beaver Lake, deep enough only for ducks, walk to the large stone farmhouse on a bridle path 10 minutes from the *belvédère* (lookout). Head for the second-floor **Centre de la Montagne** to pick up information on guided tours, thematic visits, and maps. From the *belvédère*, the route plunges through history. City founder de Maisonneuve reportedly raised a cross here in 1643, grateful that his tiny encampment had escaped a flood. That may be apocryphal, but a steel cross stands 30 meters (98 ft), lighting the Montréal sky every night since 1924. You can't miss it.

With an hour to spare and some extra energy, you can reach the cross and climb down steep stairs to a lookout on Camillien Houde parkway, 21 meters (70 ft) below. Also below are two huge cemeteries, **Mont-Royal** and **Notre-Dame-des-Neiges** (one Protestant, one Catholic), opened on farm terraces in the mid-1800s. If you want to explore later, get a map of the monuments. Here's where the city buried its notable citzens. Now, crab apple trees and Japanese lilacs attract birds and bird-watchers. There are good views from the lookout – if you can ignore the canoodling couples in parked cars. (Public morality campaigns in the 1950s led to the felling of the stands of trees that once hid romantic encounters, but young and sometimes old Montréalers are not so easily thwarted.)

'L'Ange'

To continue along the main trail, head back towards the *belvédère*.

Otherwise, skip the detour to the lookout and locate the steel-railed steps just east of the *belvédère*, climb gingerly down and link up with a bridle path, where horse-drawn *calèches* vie with joggers and city police on horseback. Just follow two cutbacks for half an hour to the trail's end, where *L'Ange* flutters at the pinnacle of the **Sir Georges-Etienne Cartier Monument** (40 meters/131 ft). If you spot her, beeline across the grass and save yourself the steps. Here, each Sunday in summer, women dance barefoot and men pound drums at 1960s-style 'tam-tams' near the Avenue du Parc entrance.

To head across town, take bus 80 or 129 down to Place-des-Arts metro station. Follow the metro lines east to Pie-IX stop. Exit the station, and head uphill on Boulevard Pie-IX toward Rue Sherbrooke.

A quick glance around will alert you to the major territory to explore, both north and south of Sherbrooke. First, head for the best lunch in the neighborhood at **Le Château Dufresne**, (tel: 259-9201) Wednesday to Sunday 10am–5pm), 2929 Jeanne d'Arc, on the corner of Sherbrooke and Pie-IX. Enter through the mansion's back door and check out the menu in the café to the left. It's tasty fare.

In the Insectarium

This was one of the city's first reinforced concrete buildings. Finished in 1918, this grand Beaux-Arts double residence belonged to two brothers. Its 44 rooms cover it all: Louis XV and Louis XVI bedrooms, Tudor and Gothic study, Classical and Renaissance dining room, Second Empire salons, Elizabethan library. Some rooms feature original furnishings. Others are galleries, where stark modernity contrasts with late 19th century frills. Note that a portion of the museum – the Musée des Arts Décoratifs – has moved to the Musée des Beaux-Arts, 1379 Sherbrooke Ouest *(see page 36 for further details)*.

Now, cross north of Sherbrooke, heading east to the lush expanse of **Jardin Botanique de Montréal** (tel: 872-1400, open daily 9am–5pm, until 7pm May to September), a huge botanical garden located at 4101 Sherbrooke Est. The collection is diverse, educational and topnotch, especially for children: 30,000 species at 30 outdoor sites and 10 themed greenhouses. Second in size only to England's Kew Gardens, this one (75 hectares/185 acres) leans towards the Oriental. It boasts the most dwarf trees and largest Chinese garden outside Asia. Nearby, the **Insectarium** includes a spectacular display of some 400,000 insects – some alive, most pinned. Exhibits pose such mind-numbing questions as 'What would our planet be like without dung-eaters?' Even the building is green and bugshaped.

Cross Sherbrooke again to **Parc Olympique**, the Olympic complex at 4141 Pierre de Coubertin that the city built when it hosted the Summer Olympics in 1976. Imaginative recycling is underway, but the concrete expanses of these Olympian mementos can be overwhelming. There's enough concrete here to lay a sidewalk to Calgary, 4,020 km (2,500 miles) west. Former mayor Jean Drapeau and French architect Roger Taillibert employed a radical technique, new in the mid-1970s: pre-formed concrete. The result is fondly dubbed Big O, less fondly Big Owe, as taxpayers are still paying off costs three decades later. Costs burgeoned from a projected $310 million to more than a billion dollars. The former head of a prominent school of architecture called it a 'monument to illusion.'

First of all, head to the **Biodôme** (daily 9am–7pm), at 4777 Pierre de Coubertin, a fascinating walkabout museum that calls itself a living slice of the planet. This venue is the former Olympic vélodrome, at one time the largest indoor cycling track in the world. Nowadays you must leave your bike outside, as the 500-meter (1,650-ft) trek through four different eco-systems is on foot. Because Montréal

At the Biodôme

winters are so cold, Biodôme's effort to bring outdoors inside may not seem that crazy. Most of what you see – cliffs, grottoes, and giant trees – is concrete: hollowed-out boulders must suffice; real ones are too heavy.

This New Age museum provides a variety of soil textures, temperatures, and humidity levels to enable 4,000 animals and 5,000 plants to feel at home. The first eco-system is perhaps the most convincing: a tropical rain

forest patterned after Costa Rica. Even in the dry season, the humidity is 70 percent, with artificial light carefully measured and mist puffed from trees. Some plants are real, others not. Some animals seem convinced by it, and others are not. It's best to visit between 4pm and 5pm, when the animals are most active.

Moving along through the different environments within the Biodôme, the marine environment offers beavers at work and otters at play. Explore woods and streams of the Laurentian forest (the real thing is only a 45-minute drive away). In the next corridor, look for penguins in 'convergent evolution' at the Arctic and Antarctic, normally 10,000 km (6,200 miles) apart. But the system is far from perfect; the sloth won't keep its two toes in the prescribed tree; the waterfall gushes too noisily. Even the museum urges: 'Go outside and discover!' But first, if you want to claim your part in the food chain, try the snack bar downstairs.

To explore the **Stade Olympique et Tour** (daily tours from 11am) you can join a train tour or walk with guides wielding megaphones. Stadium tours start with a 30-minute film offering a snapshot of

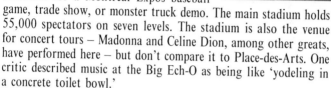

the city: multi-image, wide-screen, surround-sound, sanitized. No mention of concrete that flakes off – including one 50-tonne chunk in 1991, an inside wall in 1994. This stadium is best remembered for action. For a nominal price, you can train, swim, dive, or work out. Many Montréalers take advantage of its excellent facilities.

At the base of the tower are six pools built for Olympic competition, to warm-up, train, dive, and compete, plus a pool for scuba. Bring swimwear and dive in. Or check schedules for a Montréal Expos baseball game, trade show, or monster truck demo. The main stadium holds 55,000 spectators on seven levels. The stadium is also the venue for concert tours – Madonna and Celine Dion, among other greats, have performed here – but don't compare it to Place-des-Arts. One critic described music at the Big Ech-O as being like 'yodeling in a concrete toilet bowl.'

Don't miss the other pleasures of the complex. In just minutes, you can ride the exterior cable car up the 175-meter (575-ft) tower (tel: 868-3000, June 15 to September 2: 10am–9pm; rest of the year: 10am–6pm). The tilt at the top is 45°, though you'll still be upright. (The Tower of Pisa has only a 5.5° incline.) The tower was crowned with steel beams hoisted more than a decade after the stadium hosted Olympic triumphs. Three huge skylights provide a peek at the stadium's retractable roof and giant cable structure, which is now under constant repair. The view from the observation deck is panoramic. On a clear day, you can see for up to 80 km (50 miles). At dusk, as magical light envelops the city, look back toward the mountain where you'll see the cross beckoning, and monuments exchanging nods.

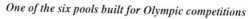

One of the six pools built for Olympic competitions

DAY 3

Museum Stroll

This full-day tour takes a look at the eclectic art museums of Sherbrooke Ouest. It begins with a buffet breakfast and ends with afternoon tea at the Ritz Carlton.

'Foule Illuminée'

—Men should wear a jacket if they want to take tea at the Ritz Carlton, as suggested. This tour starts at the McGill metro station.—

From McGill metro station, it's only a five-minute walk to Rue Sherbrooke, the city's main east—west downtown thoroughfare. Follow Avenue McGill College uphill, and look for your first street art: Raymond Mason's sculpture, *Foule Illuminée* (the Illuminated Crowd), cream-colored figures glinting against blue-black glass.

If you want a reasonably priced breakfast treat, head left to nearby Hotel Omni Mont-Royal's **Opus II** (tel: 985-6252), 1050 Sherbrooke Ouest at Rue Peel. The buffet is terrific, the setting grand and the service smooth.

Afterwards, proceed to Sherbrooke, a street for strutting. This is the edge of the **Golden Square Mile**, a neighborhood dubbed golden for the 100 prosperous residents who controlled 70 percent of Canada's wealth at the end of the 19th century. Today, what they left behind is a street flush with art galleries, pricey boutiques, luxury hotels and *antiquaires*. This is as close as Montréal gets to grand. The stately graystone homes, trimmed with turrets and huge bay windows, date from the 1890s, when the railway boom fueled a building frenzy.

To put all this in perspective, head immediately to **Musée McCord**, the Museum of Canadian History (tel: 398-7100, open Saturday and Sunday 10am–5pm, Tuesday to Friday 10am–6pm; free Saturday 10am–noon), at 690 Sherbrooke Ouest. Look for the Inukshuk, an Inuit rock statue outside. This signals more aboriginal treats inside, including a two-story cedar Haida totem. Founder David Ross McCord, an eccentric with an unfashionable fondness

McGill University

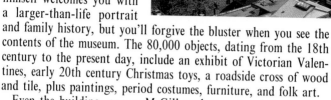

for Canadiana, emptied his own and his friends' closets to make a donation in 1919 of 15,000 pieces that laid the foundation of the ethnographic collection. McCord himself welcomes you with a larger-than-life portrait and family history, but you'll forgive the bluster when you see the contents of the museum. The 80,000 objects, dating from the 18th century to the present day, include an exhibit of Victorian Valentines, early 20th century Christmas toys, a roadside cross of wood and tile, plus paintings, period costumes, furniture, and folk art.

Even the building, once a McGill student center, is interesting. When it was expanded to twice its size, the design netted an architect's award, but you'll still find plenty of nooks and crannies. Luckily, fingers on signs point the way. Look for the work of William Notman, the Scottish immigrant who opened the city's first commercial photo studio in 1856. The third floor houses 400,000 images shot by his studios, plus 350,000 from other Canadians. These 19th-century portraits, composites, and landscapes present an intimate record of Canada. If it happened, Notman or his sons photographed it. (As you exit on the first floor, don't miss the museum's *salon de thé* and boutique.)

From here, head west along Sherbrooke. Stretching north is the 59-hectare (146-acre) **McGill University** campus, the legacy of a Scottish fur trader. Look for the Royal Victoria college, its 1895 statue to Queen Victoria weathering well. On Sherbrooke, between University and McTavish, the Roddick Gates mark the campus entrance, their metal embedded with clock faces and named for a

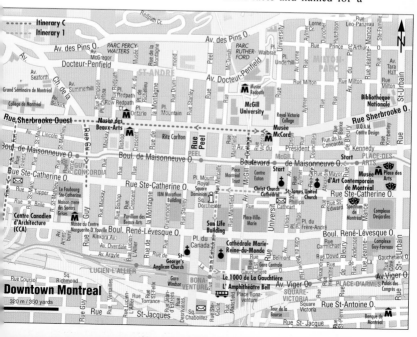

Downtown Montreal

320 m / 350 yards

The Galerie Dominion

benefactor proud of punctuality. Buildings here range from mint condition, early 19th-century to mediocre modern, with the old Arts Building dominating the horseshoe entryway. A marble fountain honors American-Canadian ties. Notice the three naked youths holding a bowl to their shoulders who have been dubbed 'The Three Bares.'

En route to the Musée des Beaux Arts, keep an eye out for the city's best art galleries. **Galerie Dominion** (tel: 845-7471), at 1438 Sherbrooke Ouest, beckons with a sidewalk parade – a Henry Moore abstract and an Auguste Rodin sculpture. Dawdle in *très chic* shops. Within a five-block area are Giorgio Armani, Versace, Sonia Rykiel, Ralph Lauren, and Emanuel Ungaro. Local pluses include Holt Renfrew, the exclusive department store with art deco architecture. Note the beaver on its copper front door on Rue de la Montagne.

At the center of all this stands Canada's oldest museum, the **Musée des Beaux-Arts** (MBA) or Museum of Fine Arts (tel: 285-1600 Tuesday to Sunday 11am–6pm, half-price for special exhibitions on Wednesday 5.30–8.30pm), at 1379 Sherbrooke Ouest, founded in 1860. A wonderful boutique, bookstore and restaurant are accessible without charge. Its exhibits are usually very good: DaVinci, Chagall, Dali, art deco, as well as Montréaler Jean-Paul Riopelle and Quebecer Jean-Paul Lemieux. Its permanent collection of 25,000 objects range from Peruvian textiles to English porcelain and Japanese incense boxes. The museum features a classical facade of white Vermont marble and sweeping staircases to its 3.6-meter (12-ft) front doors. This museum also includes the **Musée des Arts Décoratifs**, the only North American museum to focus exclusively on international design from

The Musée des Beaux-Arts

1935 – glass, textiles, ceramics, furniture. You will find works by Frank Lloyd Wright as well as more whimsical offerings: drawings of Babar the elephant, lace from Belgium, and National Geographic photos taken all over the world. But despite recent renovations, the Musée des Beaux-Arts is showing its age. The lighting in particular can be poor.

Across the street to the south, stunningly modern by contrast, is the MBA's **pavilion** (1380 Sherbrooke Ouest). Designed by Montréal architect Moshe Safdie, the seven stories (five above ground) are an exciting blend of old and new. It's almost irrelevant what's on display. Consider the building as art and look hard. A 12-meter (40-ft) gateway invites you to the lobby. The glass roof rises obliquely from the second to fifth floor, flooding the entrance hall with light. Don't miss the glassed-in sculpture garden on the fourth floor. It offers breath-taking views, a blend of neo-Gothic churches, Victorian houses and 1950s office buildings.

For lunch or afternoon tea, backtrack to Le Jardin du Ritz at the **Ritz Carlton Montréal** (tel: 842-4212, ext 759), 1228 Sherbrooke Ouest at Drummond (men must wear a jacket). The garden – open only in summer – is delightful, with a dozen ducklings frolicking in the courtyard pond. Afternoon tea is served from 3.30–5pm, English-style with scones and cream or Continental-style with sandwiches and pastries. Thus fortified, you might consider walking as far west along Sherbrooke as Rue du Fort, where a Sulpician seminary still hunkers behind massive fieldstone walls. Its two Martello towers still stand firm, originally intended to protect Indian converts as long ago as 1683.

Afterwards you can head home, backtracking to Rue Guy and down to Guy-Concordia metro (if you're still hungry, pass beyond the metro to Rue Ste-Catherine and Le Faubourg at 1616, where 60 food stalls – fruit, vegetables and

Welcome to the Ritz

fancy imports – fill three floors). Alternatively, for an esoteric treat, turn south for a 10-minute walk on Rue du Fort to CCA, the **Centre Canadien d'Architecture** (tel: 939-7000, open June to September: Tuesday to Sunday 11am–6pm, Thursday to 9pm; October to May: Wednesday and Friday 11am–6pm, Thursday to 9pm; Saturday and Sunday 11am–5pm), at 1920 Baile. Admission is free on Thursday after 5.30pm. The CCA can be intimidatingly academic but its setting is an architectural plus: an elegantly restored, 19th-century mansion wedded to sleek modern wings. The staircase sweeps you into an airy space. With many exhibits a year, CCA explores all aspects of architecture: its art, history, and impact. It has 150,000 drawings, photographs, and books, some dating from the 15th century. Afterwards, cross Boulevard René Lévesque to a unique sculpture park.

1. Founding influences: Fur and Church

A morning combining two very different sides of Montréal – the city's bustling fur district and some of the city's grand old churches. Plus rest and relaxation at the ice rink. See map on page 35.

–To reach the start of this tour, take the metro to Place-des-Arts.–

From Place-des-Arts metro, walk west two blocks along Boulevard de Maisonneuve. Here you will find construction debris, neglected grass, parking lots, and exquisite fur coats, dozens of them, carried or rolled on racks, in the city's **district de la fourrure** (furrier's district). Even if you can't imagine yourself buying or wearing fur, a visit to the district's four-square blocks will illustrate how fur has played a central role in Montréal's heritage and culture. Nearly 85 percent of Canada's annual $800 million business happens here.

Start at **Grosvenor's**, at 390 de Maisonneuve Ouest, a furrier who helped establish fur's glamor in the 1980s, when Victor Skrebneski photos advertised cool beauties wearing lavish minks, hats, gloves and little else. This street-level store and **McComber Furs**, at 440 de Maisonneuve Ouest, are large and well established. Smaller competitors line Rue Mayor, running parallel one block south. If you're feeling adventurous, explore the high-rise **Sommer**, at 416 de Maisonneuve. Look for the ground-floor signs announcing upstairs furriers.

Browsing is easy. Some 200 small, family-run fur companies are located here, along Rue de Bleury, St-Alexandre, and Mayor. You'll quickly find furs to fondle. Sales staff are continually telling customers that the furs are 100 percent natural, non-polluting, biodegradable, to fend off anti-fur forces. Some sell by order; others, usually those on the ground floor, carry inventory. Ask for a personal tour of workshops. With smaller pelts, especially mink, notice how they are lengthened by intricate 'letting out.' Enjoy *l'esprit du manteau* that designers add to sporty styles or elegant classics – for example, the vibrant colors, jagged edges, and signature linings from Montréaler Zuki Balaila, Canada's premier designer.

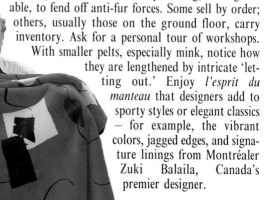

Wrap up in a Zuki Balaila design

Gothic St James

From the fur district, walk south along City Councillors to **Rue Ste-Catherine**, once the city's top commercial thoroughfare, but now distinctly tawdry. Ste-Catherine supports the claim that Montréal has more churches and topless bars per capita than any other city. Look along the north side of the street for a steeple towering above the neon. This is the stately Gothic facade of **St James' United Church** (tel: 288-9245), 463 Ste-Catherine Ouest. Finished in 1890, the Methodist church features horseshoe pews, ceiling rosettes, and an appealing sanctuary. The doors stay open on weekdays from mid-May to September. Listen for free organ recitals on Tuesdays at 12.30pm, and test the seat cushions stuffed with horse-hair.

Look both ways along Ste-Catherine. With one glance you'll notice the odd mix of crass and class. To the east, for example, look for **Séduction**, at 38 Ouest. With two sprawling floors, this may indeed be the biggest sex shop in North America, as it claims. If so, it follows a tradition set by this street in the 19th century, in size if not in content. Then, all Montréal's *grands magasins* were located here, and many major department stores still remain. If you walk west, you find the traditional: **The Bay**, at No 585 and **Ogilvy**, at No 1307 (the only thing not muted at this department store is the restaurant's bagpiper, clad in Ogilvy tartan, pipes covered with red plaid). En route is **Birks**, 1240 Carré Phillips at Ste-Catherine, supplier of fine jewelry in treasured blue boxes. Its lovely interior has hardly changed since 1894.

Pause for an ice cream

The landmark department store, Eaton's, also located on this street, has sold its last wares and closed its doors. While its future in the city is uncertain, the adjacent Eaton Centre complex of shops remains. It's a combination of tacky, sexy, and overpriced clubwear, footwear and lingerie, with the odd eatery and linen store tucked in as well.

Or continue west to collide with **Square Dorchester**, Montréal's downtown landmark for a century. Look for **Infotouriste** to the north, between Rue Metcalfe and Rue Peel. If you have travel questions, step in. City tour buses leave from here. The square itself is filled with lunch-munchers, pigeons and statuary commemorating British imperialism. A horseman honors Boer War heroes. A fountain commemorates Queen Victoria's 1897 diamond jubilee. By 1879, this square featured six churches, prompting guides to cite

Cathédrale Marie-Reine-du-Monde

the eminently quotable American visitor Mark Twain: 'This is the first time I was ever in a city where you couldn't throw a brick without breaking a church window.'

Now, only two churches remain. On the southeast corner reigns **Cathédrale Marie-Reine-du-Monde**, Mary Queen of the World Cathedral, the archdiocese's neo-baroque basilica finished in 1894. If it looks vaguely familiar, it's supposed to. It's a quarter-scale model of St Peter's in Rome, and even the fresco under the canopy is a faithful copy of Bernini's. The paintings inside are grim and somber: larger-than-life pictures of martyrdom, at the stake and in the rapids. Patron saints of local parishes line the roof. Nearby, at 1101 Stanley, is **St George's Anglican Church**, honoring England's patron saint. Built in 1870, it is one of Canada's finest examples of Gothic revival architecture.

To the east is a temple of a different sort – a granite monolith, the former headquarters of Sun Life Insurance Company, and once the biggest building in the British Empire. Built in three stages over 20 years, it rises 26 floors and dips three. The day the Parti Québécois came to power, Sun Life announced its departure for Toronto. Its carillons still ring at 5pm, however, marking time for businesses that stayed. Indeed, two new business symbols soar nearby. The IBM Marathon building, at 1250 René Lévesque Ouest, offers an interior garden towering to 25 meters (81 ft), and Montréal's tallest office building, **Le 1000 de la Gauchetière**, stretching 51 stories. Here, on the mezzanine, is an ice rink, **L'Amphitheatre Bell** (daily 11:30am–6pm, shorter hours on Tuesday). Don a pair of rented skates and glide along, joining the suits on their lunch break.

Skating at L'Amphitheatre Bell

2. Boulevard St-Laurent

A morning walk along the ethnically mixed Boulevard St-Laurent, plus chic to schlock shops. See map on page 43.

—Take the metro to St-Laurent station, and leave by the only exit.—

No subtlety here, **Boulevard St-Laurent** screams for attention. 'Boulevard' is too refined; its nickname, *La Main* (The Main), will do. The street divides francophone *Est* from anglophone *Ouest*, but it also unites. Note the bilingual graffiti. Indeed all cultures and ages convene, rather than clash, here. In the next dozen blocks, you'll discover allophone Montréal distilled.

This is not a street to tread lightly. Gridlock is constant, as drivers zigzag, cyclists scramble, and strollers jaywalk. At the beginning of the 20th century, few people lived north of Sherbrooke, and the Main welcomed Sunday strollers who arrived by trolley. Then, immigrants – Eastern European Jews, Chinese, Greeks, Italians – got off boats and headed up the block, staying only until they could afford to leave. The street turned from chic to the Depression's skid row.

As you wander up, you'll find traces of this cultural melting-pot everywhere: kosher butchers, Hungarian bakeries, Portuguese shops crammed with kitsch. Sniff out food shops and restaurants, first-rate and fast-rate.

Of course, you'll get distracted. Start in the 3400 block. Here, avant garde boutiques flank trendy restaurants. For The Main's peculiar *mélange*, check the 3600 block. **Chez Barateiro Portugais**, a tailor at 3650, nestles near sophisticated luggage at 3662 and hardware bins at 3664.

If the Old World beckons, head north, and indulge your senses. 'Little Europe' butcher shops cram two blocks (**Hoffner** at No 3671 is a good example). There are many more as well – all of which are perfect

Shopping on St-Laurent

places to pick up that authentically obscure French mustard, Swiss cheese, German chocolate or tin of Danish smoked herring you just wouldn't be able to find anywhere else. **Boulangerie St-Laurent**, at No 3830, one of the city's oldest bakeries, churns out *challahs* (plaited loaves of bread) and Russian rye, its brick ovens sizzling since 1912. Don't pass up the gooey cinnamon buns. **La Vieille Europe**, at No 3855, offers racks of sausages, mounds of cheeses, pleasing pastas and *pâtés*. The chocolate deserves serious attention.

Delve into a deli

Here, on The Main, discover smoked meat, beef brisket Montréal-style. **Schwartz**, at No 3895, sets the high standard, with delicious meat which is smoked on the premises. If the area is too elbow-to-elbow for you, cross the street to **The Main**, at No 3864, which is open 24 hours. In either place, prepare to forget cholesterol levels.

The next block – as Napoleon, Bagg and St-Laurent collide – is the neighborhood's heart. On the northwest corner, at No 3950, stands **Schubert Baths**, built in 1931. To the southwest, **L Berson & Fils**, at No 3884, make headstones and monuments strong enough and long enough to support four generations. Southeast, at No 3953, is **Simcha's Fruit** *marché*, a quintessential cornershop telling neighborhood tales. From here, consider climbing the stairs, at No 3961, to **Moishes** (tel: 845-3509), where the city's more memorable steaks have been served since 1937. Here you can nosh on appetizers and daily specials to your heart's (and stomach's) content.

If you prefer, instead of making a beeline north, you can explore with jaunts east or west. Head one block west to Clark, for the first non-Catholic place of worship in Montréal, the **Spanish and Portuguese synagogue** at Bagg and Clark. Or consider a dash down Prince Arthur, a haven for hippies in the 1960s and '70s and these days a pedestrian mall with restaurants inviting you to

apportez votre vin (bring your own wine). In warm weather, carnival prevails here, with musicians and jugglers frolicking among outdoor diners. Continue eight blocks east and you'll be on solidly French St-Denis, cultures away. Or you can follow Napoleon east to Laval, north to Duluth, and back to St-Laurent.

The Main attracts literature and art, practitioners and patrons. Though you might not come across poet-singer-neighbor Leonard Cohen, you might meet a poetry-reading protégé. Creativity ferments in second-or-third-floor studios, lofts, and galleries that fill old office buildings. **The Balfour**, at No 3575, and **Cooper** at No 3981, offer space for artists. The names of shops and bars tend

Character housing off The Main

to reflect dreams rather than reality. **Café Ciné-Lumière** at No 5163, and the huge, hip and happening complex known as **Cinéma Ex-Centris**, (tel: 847-3536), No 3536, with its **Café Méliès** (tel: 847-9218), allow customers to sip soups and drinks as they relax and enjoy the films.

The 'old neighborhood' stays north of Roy. To the west, *poissonnerie* **Waldman** at 76 Roy Est (tel: 285-8747), one of the city's oldest and largest fish sellers, has expanded further. New Greek owners opened **Waldman Plus** (entrance round the corner at 76 Avenue des Pins Est), with smoked fish and fish and chips, to take out or eat in. *Fala portugues? Parla italiano? Habla español?* Start learning the languages now, as first-generation Portuguese patronize banks, shops, and diners here today, just as other nationalities did yesterday. **Jano** (tel: 849-0646), at No 3883, specializes in barbecues traditional in Portugal's Ribatejo, and **Coco Rico** (tel: 849-5554), at No 3907, offers tasty chicken sandwiches, roasted potatoes and cornbread. Shops here are full of Portuguese products: tabloids, glazed pottery, roosters for luck, plus travel agents packaging the Azores. The immigrant tradition of saving money and sending it home is very strong.

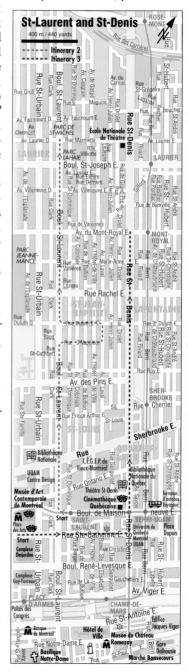

If you peek around corners here, you'll discover old men nursing cold beers, while studying European soccer scores. Listen for the sad strains of Portuguese *fado* music, live or piped. If you venture along parallel streets, Coloniale to the east or Clark to the west, you'll discover houses painted in vivid hues, a mania that the Portuguese started in the 1970s.

But the Portuguese have claimed this neighborhood with more than paint. On holidays, distinctive parades careen through these side streets. Check out **Parc Portugal**, at the corner of Marie-Anne, for a *padrao* monument erected by Portuguese explorers. Yet even here, you see signs

Hand-held gems

of newer immigrants from Central and South America. **Parc des Amériques** at Rachel offers Aztec designs.

Even if there's a feel of urban no-man's-land for a block or two, you're safe. Gentrification is not far. Antique shops sprout and grow more eclectic as you travel north. As you near Avenue Laurier, you will notice that high-roller franco-phones from nearby Outremont take over the scene. **La Cage aux Soldes** tempts with designer discounts at No 5120.

If your energy is waning and you need to recharge, stop off at **Café Kilo**, at No 5602. Rue St-Denis in the heart of the city or the streets of the Franco-Jewish suburb, Outremont are the two of the best places to sample the local java. There is so much choice in this *café au lait* city.

To find a metro to take you back to base, walk west two blocks to St-Urbain and catch bus 55 south to St-Laurent station. Or walk east eight blocks to St-Denis, where you will find metro stops every five blocks.

3. Contemporary Culture

An afternoon stroll through modern Montréal, taking in contem-porary art and a thriving university district. Plus the cafés and shops on St-Denis. See map on page 43.

—Take the metro to Place-des-Arts.—

From Place-des-Arts metro station, follow underground signs to one of Canada's first modern art museums, the **Musée d'Art Contemporain de Montréal** (tel: 847-6226, Tuesday to Sunday 11am–6pm, free Wednesday 6–9pm), at 185 Ste-Catherine Ouest. Near the entrance, look for sculptor Pierre Granche's *Comme si le temps ... de la rue.*

The museum offers an overview of *Québécois* art from the late 1930s, punctuated with Canadian, European and American works. Quebec artists dominate the museum's 5,000 works, including many abstracts: abstract expressionism, geometric abstraction and post-pictorial abstraction. Some pieces signal Quebec's struggle for identity. Even the museum's inconsistent signage – always French, some-times French-English – reflects this.

Up sweeping stairs to the north, look for temporary exhibits of video art or photography. To the south are selections from the museum's permanent collection: 200 pieces that include works by Warhol, Dubuffet, Picasso, Lichtenstein, and nationally known Alfred Pellan and Paul Emile-Borduas. In summer, explore the outdoor sculpture garden. On the way out, check Artexte bookstore, the museum boutique, and Bell's Info-Arts center.

Now you have choices. If you want more art, head south to Rue Ste-Catherine and its private galleries, in particular the high-rise

Gallery on St-Denis

at 372 Ste-Catherine Ouest (Tuesday to Saturday 10am–5pm), which houses about a dozen. Or just head east to **Rue St-Denis**, a street filled with sidewalk cafés, intimate restaurants, and rows of Victorian graystones.

North along St-Denis is the city's **Latin Quarter**. In the 1920s, the Université de Montréal fostered an intellectual and cultural elite of French Canadians. Today, the atmosphere is tied to the Université du Québec à Montréal (UQAM) – pizza palaces, bars, and La Capoterie (No 2061), which sells humorous condoms. But it's still a preserve of Québécois culture: bookstores, art galleries, Théâtre St-Denis at No 1545 (where Sarah Bernhardt performed), even the imposing Bibliothèque Nationale du Québec, at 1700.

UQAM, at No 1455, features the **St-Jacques Tower**, the city's highest building when constructed in 1880 and a designated historic site since 1973. Check out art-house screenings at **La Cinémathèque Québécoise** (tel: 842-9763), 335 de Maisonneuve Est, or the ONF/National Film Board (tel: 496-6887), at 1564 St-Denis. A high-tech NFB robot slots your laser-disc choices from over 8,000 films.

Pause on a park bench or patch of grass at Carré St-Louis, where Sherbrooke and St-Denis intersect. Its majestic graystones housed francophone writers and artists at the end of the 19th century. Here, you can do what *les Montréalais* do best: choose a view, sit and watch the world go by. For Montréalers, people-watching is a passionate pursuit. If it's warm, someone may jump in the fountain. Don't be put off by panhandling or propositioning.

Or choose a café. Try **L'Express** (tel: 845-5333), at No 3927, as enticing as any Parisian bistro. Grab a seat by the window or under the domed skylight in the back. **Café Cherrier** (tel: 843-4308), nearby at No 3635, is for intellectualizing. Or stop for a sip of coffee at **La Brûlerie St-Denis** (tel: 286-9158), at No 3967

Café society

Typical spiral staircase

(other branches at No 1587 and else-where across the city).

Ready to stretch? Head north, as far as Avenue du Mont-Royal, and enjoy pretty residences transformed into specialty boutiques. Look up to see ornate Victorian cornices, windows and exterior staircases, in copper, slate and gray limestone. Off St-Denis, narrow side streets such as Villeneuve and Gilford turn at odd angles. Admire outdoor staircases on Rue St-Hubert, which runs parallel east of St-Denis. It's worth the side trip, if only to contemplate how residents manage through icy stretches. 'We've learned how to fall without breaking our backs,' one confided.

Serious shopping along St-Denis is best tackled in the afternoon. Many stores do not open until 11am or noon, but stay open as late as 9pm, especially on Thursday, Friday, and holidays. Despite the fashionable address, turnover is high. You will notice that specialty shops often come in pairs located across from each other: two shops for hats, two for home furnishings, two for papers and pens. Resist the temptation to cross mid-block. You don't want to be another traffic statistic: drivers are fast and unpredictable.

As well as offering some rather unusual shops, this is also the best stretch of St-Denis on which to find a wide range of items, such as high-quality cookware, travel books, jewelry and (of course) up-to-the-minute fashions.

If you're hungry, you're in the right place. Tough competition keeps prices reasonable and choices varied. The ethnic reach is spectacular, drawing influences from the province and abroad. In

blocks on and around St-Denis, you'll find Belgian, Mexican, Thai, Spanish, Brazilian, Acadian, and *nouvelle* French Canadian. The side street policy of *apportez votre vin* (bring your own wine) has slipped onto St-Denis itself. At dusk, the street pulses to the beat of non-stop nightlife. Some spots take an innovative approach. **Kamikaze Curiosities** (tel: 848-0728), at No 4156, sells funky jewelry from Canadian designers by day but, by night, rolls its display cases away to make way for a club, **Le Passeport** (tel: 842-6063). It's certainly popular, so be assured, night or day, the street is always jammed.

Good companions

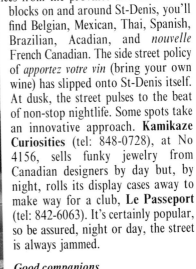

4. Expo Islands

Cut loose to the islands in the middle of the St Lawrence river. On a sunny afternoon, you can swim, cycle, picnic, paddle, or just daydream.

–Take the metro to Ile Ste-Hélène or a shuttle or water taxi from the Old Port, or a taxi across Pont Jacques Cartier or Pont de la Concorde. In the summer, a free shuttle near the metro will ferry you to major sites. Alternatively, you can look for the helpful map posted outside the metro station, and walk.–

In 1967, when the World's Fair drew 53 million visitors to Montréal, two man-made islands in the St Lawrence river, Ile Ste-Hélène and Ile Notre-Dame, became the playground for 'Man and His World.' But when **Expo '67**'s glory and buildings faded, the islands became the city's best-kept secret, a pleasant escape from summer heat and bustle. Then, in 1993, Loto-Québec opened a casino that changed all that. The rush is on *(see Pick & Mix 5, page 49)*. But even if gambling doesn't interest you, **Parc Jean-Drapeau** is well worth an afternoon's visit.

Explore **Ile Ste-Hélène** first. If you can resist the three swimming pools near the metro, plot a route to the island's eastern tip first. Here is the province's largest amusement park, **La Ronde** (tel: 872-4537, open 11am–11pm, mid-May to early September. The 55-hectare (135-acre) park offers more than 30 rides, plus one of the world's highest wooden dual-track roller-coasters. Carnival atmosphere dominates, with lines longest at the newest thrills. On weekends in June and July, international firework competitions light up the night.

Alternatively, follow *Le Fort* signs for a history lesson. The fort was built in 1822 on the orders of the Duke of Wellington. It served as a hospital in the cholera epi-

Looping the loop at La Ronde

demic in 1830 and as a prisoner-of-war camp in World War II. Amid arsenal, blockhouse and powder magazine, the **David M Stewart Museum** (tel: 861-6701, Wednesday to Monday 10am–5pm, to 6pm Thursday and Friday in summer) offers a fascinating look at the history of European exploration and New France. Named for its founder, heir to a tobacco fortune, the museum offers a selection of 30,000 artifacts – firearms, tools, scientific instruments, old maps, rare books and a worthy insight into the people who used them. Whether you prefer the ordinary, such as a recreated kitchen with bread oven, or the extraordinary (a Gobelin tapestry with a fictitious twist) it's here.

Traditional crafts

Sometimes the museum hosts workers practicing traditional crafts. You may see pewter spoons, beeswax Baby Jesuses, or *flechée ceinturon* – belts worn by Hudson's Bay Company trappers – being made. During summer, wait for 18th-century military drills of La Compagnie Franche de la Marine and the 78th Fraser Highlanders, (performed Wednesday to Sunday 11am, 1pm, 3pm and 4.30pm). For 45 minutes, drill teams dressed like troops once garrisoned here fix bayonets and fire a 320-kg (700-lb) cannon.

Now, head to Ste-Hélène's western tip to see the distinctive Expo '67 sculptures. Examine Alexander Calder's *Man*, his second largest stabile and the only one unpainted, or Buckminster Fuller's geodesic dome, the former US pavilion which is now the **Biosphère**, an interesting environmental observation centre focusing on the ecosystem of the Great Lakes.

Follow walkways or grab a bus to **Ile Notre-Dame**. Here you can picnic (bring your own blanket), hire pedal boats, wind-surf, cycle along shady trails, or swim. The artificial **beach** – fresh water, not salt; pigeons, not seagulls – is a short distance from the St Lawrence (which is too polluted with PCBs and mercury for swimming). Even crammed to capacity with 5,000 sun-worshippers, the beach is peaceful: no food or boom-boxes allowed on the beach itself. Nor bottles, so bring canned drinks.

If you don't wish to swim, roam through the **Jardin de Floralies**, created in 1980 when Montréal became the first North American city to host a world horticultural show. Look for the rare taiga display. Admission is free.

The island also offers at least two notable restaurants for dinner. **Hélène de Champlain** (tel: 395-2424), at 200 Tour de l'Ile, has outdoor terraces set amid roses and greenery. Close to the fort, **Le Festin du Gouverneur** (tel: 879-1141) offers four courses at a 17th-century-style banquet.

En route back to the metro, you're likely to encounter a festival. The former Olympic rowing basin hosts dragon boat races in May, a Grand Prix in June, a gastronomic feast in August. You might even stumble into a concert – classical or rock music – and 75,000 other people sprawled on top of a grassy knoll near the metro.

A picnic on Ile Ste-Hélène

The Casino with its wrap-around windows

5. Le Casino de Montréal

A night-time jaunt to Ile Notre-Dame, home to Loto-Québec's first casino, the hugely popular Le Casino de Montréal. Join the casino's regulars and try your luck.

—Take the metro to Ile Ste-Hélène or take a taxi. Parking is a headache, so leave cars behind.—

From the metro station follow the concrete bridge to neighboring Ile Notre-Dame, where the French Expo '67 pavilion has been converted into **La Casino de Montréal** (daily 24 hours; no admission or tips; tel: 392-2746 or 1 800-665 2274 toll free).

Las Vegas glitz or Mediterranean chic? More hotel lobby than pleasure palace, the casino features natural light, not neon. Patrons are well-dressed and well-behaved. They are expected to follow certain rules: no jeans, running shoes or jogging pants are allowed, and no drinking whilst betting. The crowds are intense, lending truth to the rumor that the people of Quebec have a penchant for gambling. Since the opening of the casino in 1993, locals have crammed in, making seats — even the most expensive ones — hard to find at the blackjack tables. Each day, 1,000 players immediately fill spots at 1,700 slot machines and 100 gaming tables for blackjack, midi-baccarat, and roulette.

When you arrive, be prepared to wait a while before finding room at one of the tables. Week nights are definitely less crowded than weekends, when even the slot machine that takes $500 tokens goes non-stop.

Before you *faites vos jeux* (place your bets) or plunk a quarter in a 'yellow bandit,' have a good look round. Wrap-around windows offer stunning views of the St Lawrence river and city. At dusk, small lights transform these islands into a fairyland.

Who plays? Almost everybody aged 18 and over pumps loonies – dollar coins – into slot machines. Fans hover near Royal Ascot, an electronic race track with racing mini-mounts. Low-tab Keno players eye numbers on electronic boards. Commands in French dominate play, but the casino staff are bilingual, and your money will speak – whatever language you use.

If the gambling doesn't grab you, enjoy live music in the lounge or browse through a boutique filled with items *fait à Québec*. No matter how late you stay, you won't starve: there's *haute cuisine* at Les Nuances, a popularly priced buffet at La Bonne Carte, a snack bar, plus real bars on each floor. If you become obsessed, call the gambler's hot-line or rely on the casino's self-exclusion policy. If you win, enjoy – it's tax-free in Canada.

6. Spectator Sports

Do as the Montréalers do and enjoy an evening watching hockey (Les Canadiens at the Molson Centre) or baseball (Les Expos at the Olympic stadium).

Depending on whether your choice of game is hockey or baseball (this may depend on the season; *see page 51*), take the metro to Bonaventure for the Molson Centre, 1260 Rue de la Gauchetière West or Pie-IX station for the stadium; tel: 932-2582; visit: www.centremolson.com. Night games begin at 7.30pm; 8pm for hockey).

For ice-hard proof that not all Canadians are peace keepers, grab a rinkside seat at a Montréal Canadiens game. Remember these facts: Montréalers aren't sports fans; they're fanatics. Hockey isn't merely the national pastime; it's the national passion. *Les Canadiens* aren't just heroes; they're gods. So constant, so dominant is hockey in the life of Montréal's average citizen that even artists

Ice-hockey: the national passion

Baseball is second favorite

and writers have celebrated it. Season ticket-holders bequeath in their wills their seats for *Les Habs* (the nickname – derived from Les Habitants – given to Les Canadiens) lest family feuds erupt at funerals.

Each season Les Canadiens play approximately 40 home games at the Molson Centre arena. After an October opener, the season may extend as late as June, but seats are still hard to acquire. Go in person to the box office the afternoon before a game, Usually only blue seats, levels 400 and 500, or standing-room-only tickets are available by this late stage. For the best view, try for red seats, or white ones in corners; you may be lucky. If you fail to secure a ticket you may want to console yourself with every team souvenir imaginable at the fan-o-mania boutique in Atwater station.

Less exalted, but still beloved, are the Expos, Montréal's National League baseball team. You can see any of more than 80 home games played from April through October at the Olympic Stadium, 4545 Pierre de Coubertin, tel: 252-4614; www.stadianet.com. Francophone fans give the jargon of this sport peculiar twists. A grand slam is known as a *grand chelem*, a pincher-hitter is a *frappeur d'urgence*, and, instead of 'Boo!' angry fans shout 'shoo!' Whatever the language, the Expos provide the off-season fix of sport for Les Canadiens addicts. Tickets are readily available if you turn up in person at the stadium box office (tel: 846-3976). Your best bet is to try for a seat in levels 200 or 500 but the stadium rarely sells out completely.

Soft ball in the park

Tickets to see both Les Canadiens and Les Expos in action are also available if you go in person to admission ticket booths at The Bay. They can also be booked by phone through the Admission Network (tel: 790-1245, 1-800-361-4595 (toll free from Canada), 1-800-678-5440 (toll free from US).

There's more: a stroll through any neighborhood will turn up lively, sometimes even heated, 'pick-up games'. If it's summer, you're likely to stumble into a baseball or a soccer game. During fall, *shinny* (pick-up) hockey is the favorite sporting pastime, with many Montréal youngsters fancying themselves as the next 'Rocket' Richard.

Excursions

See map on page 4.

7. To the west of the Island

A journey, by car or cycle, to the western tip of the island, taking in Canal de Lachine, a fur museum, a sculpture park, a farm and an arboretum. See map on page 4.

Join the city's avid cyclists

Cyclists can follow an easy and safe 12.5-km (8-mile) paved path along the Canal de Lachine to Lac St-Louis, from where the route joins slow-paced country lanes to Ste-Anne. Bikes can be rented at the Old Port. For information on biking in Montréal, call Vélo-Quebec, tel: 521-8356; visit: www.velo.qu.ca), located at Maison des Cyclistes, 1251 Rachel Street Est. Montréalers are avid cyclists, owners of an estimated 1 million bikes. The route outlined here is especially popular on summer weekends. Call Parks Canada (tel: 283-6054) for more information.

Begin in Old Montréal at the intersection of Rue de la Commune and Mill, and stop for breakfast or provisions just 2 km (1 mile) farther on at **Marché Atwater**, 138 Atwater, near metro station Lionel Groulx. The landmark clock tower signals the market – home to 60 produce sellers, from farmers to flower growers. If you are traveling by car, take Autoroute 20 west to the 32nd Avenue exit, and then head south (left) to Victoria Street, and turn east (right) onto Victoria until 10th Avenue, where you should turn south (right) again to Boulevard St-Joseph. Turn west (right) on St-Joseph. Free parking is available at the Musée du Commerce de la Fourrure.

The canal flows past late 19th century factories and mills to the village of Lachine. In the 1660s fur traders and explorers faced rapids so wild that they frequently had to turn back or laboriously carry canoes. The **Canal de Lachine**, completed in 1825, allowed ships to navigate upriver on the St Lawrence. This opened Montréal's routes to interior waterways and fueled the city's industrial revolution with steam power for mills and factories. After 1959, when the St

Marché Atwater

Lawrence Seaway opened, recreation largely replaced commerce.

The first stop in Lachine is the **Lieu Historique National du Commerce de la Fourrure** (April 1 to mid-October, daily 10am–12.30pm and 1–6pm; mid-October to mid-December Wednesday to Sunday 9.30am–12.30pm and 1–5pm; closed December, to March 31), at 1255 St-Joseph. Built in 1803, this Hudson's Bay Company stone shed was one of 40 warehouses that held trade goods and pelts. Now a Parks Canada Historic Site, it recreates the glory days of the nation's fur trade.

For fans of contemporary art, Lachine offers 32 outdoor sculptures, at least a dozen in **Parc René Lévesque** along the jetty near the museum. Others pop up in town parks, which are discovered en route to restaurants – Chinese, Italian and more – along St Joseph near and beyond 17th Street. However, I recommend that you eat in Ste-Anne *(see below)*.

By cycle or car, head west along **Bord-du-Lac**, Lakeshore Road. The name of the road changes at least eight times in its course, and the road wanders inland at points, but don't worry. Keep the water to your left, hugging the shoreline to the tip of the island. The road offers architectural surprises at every bend: Victorian houses, traditional French-Canadian farmhouses with sloping roofs, and spectacular modern designs. **Stewart Hall** (for opening hours, tel: 630-1221), at 176 Lakeshore, Pointe-Claire, recalls estate life in the early 1900s. This 72-room manor of a Scottish colonel is now a cultural center. You might hear classical guitar or baroque chamber music in regularly scheduled concerts.

Enjoy a promenade in **Ste-Anne**. In summer, a cheerful atmosphere prevails along the boardwalk, where teens and pensioners mix amiably. On weekends, as many as 30 yachts pull in and stoke up barbecues here. If there's time, you can join a **Croisières Bellevue** cruise around Lac St Louis or the Lac de Deux Montagnes

Lachine fur trade museum

A welcome cappuccino

that leaves from Ste-Anne lock, facing city hall (tel: 457-5245).

Although you may want to check out the restaurants that line the narrow main street, have a look at the 18th-century Simon Fraser house tucked under a bridge to the west (Fraser was a partner in the Northwest Fur Company). Volunteers of the Victorian Order of Nurses run a non-profit-making restaurant here, **Au Petit Café** (Monday to Friday 11.30am–2pm; tel: 457-5121), serving steak-and-kidney pie and other British specialties. Order homemade desserts first, because they go fast. If you want something more elegant, consider the fine Italian and exotic international cuisine at **La Strata** (tel: 457-3584), 132 Ste-Anne. There's a terrace for summer lunches and a pianist at night.

If you have time and the inclination, you may want to follow Highway 20 west, past Ste-Anne, to **Ile Perrot** (caution: if you're cycling, this is a 12-hectare/30-acre area, and no casual detour) to see **Pointe-du-Moulin** (mid-May to late August 9am–sunset, September to mid-October noon–6pm), a windmill built in 1702.

Now backtrack to Au Petit Café in Ste-Anne. For winded cyclists, this may be the end of the line. Check the train schedule for departures to Montréal's Windsor station. You can load your bike for no extra charge on the train and metro (but not during rush hour). For drivers, more outdoor treats beckon nearby, and you can try one or all. Each is tied to education, but that shouldn't spoil the fun. Head west on Rue Ste-Anne, looping under Highway 20 to Rue St-Pierre, where you turn left. Then veer right onto the Highway 40 service road. Take the first right through a cornfield to MacDonald College. Turn right just before the bridge over Highway 20. This leads to the main office of **MacDonald's Farm** (due to re-open after extensive renovation at the end of 2001).

The farm is named for tobacco king Sir William MacDonald, who bought the 230-hectare (570-acre) farm in 1905 and later donated it to the university. Pigs, lambs, geese, chickens, and ducks make this a popular petting zoo for children. Guided bilingual tours finish with a glass of cold milk.

For a quiet afternoon in a forest, head next to the **Morgan Arboretum** (tel: 398 7811, open daily 9am–4pm), at 150 Chemin des Pins. Just head out of the farm, turning left towards Trans Canada Highway 40, but taking the first right before you reach it, over the Highway 40 overpass. Continue until stopped by an *arrêt* sign, and head straight in.

MacDonald's Farm inmate

Acquired in 1945 for research, this forest is large enough to get lost in – 245 hectares (600 acres), with 40 hectares (100 acres) of plantations and specimens. Ecology trails are signposted in French, though written English guides are available. Some trails are very short, following designated 'chipmunk' or 'fox' for just 1 km (½ mile). Look for maple bark bitten by squirrels in search of sap. The best time to visit is April to May, or August to September: mosquitoes can be ferocious in summer, and in winter, the two parking lots are jammed with cars belonging to cross-country skiers.

These woodlands originally belonged to the family farm of Montréal merchant James Morgan. A third of the 150 species are indigenous: maple, hickory, ash, basswood, hemlock. Indeed, as the first certified tree farm in Quebec, the arboretum includes every tree native to Canada. A birch trail blooms from seeds collected from across Canada in 1960.

Woodlands home

For another eco-treat, head to the St Lawrence Valley **Ecomuseum** (tel: 457-9449, daily 9am–4pm) at 21, 125 Chemin Ste-Marie. As you leave the arboretum, turn left (east) at the stop sign. Look for the entrance 1 km (½ mile) away on the left. You will discover ponds, woods, marshes and meadows here. Walk through an aviary for waterfowl, over a pond for turtles and ducks, and gingerly past a snake pit, near an underwater observation post. Look for 40 species, from salamander, to black bear. This is a unique glimpse of local flora and fauna over 11 hectares (27 acres), modeled on a conservation project first tested in the southwest US.

A reclaimed marshland, this center is built from landfill and highway refuse. This is not your average zoo. Only moats separate animals and visitors. Enjoy the hands-on exhibits in the reception center and the playground at the entrance, lovingly created from inner tubes, scrap wood, and a boat no longer seaworthy. Don't miss duck releases in November or frog calls in May that draw more than 200 people – and who knows how many ducks and frogs.

For the fast track back to Montréal, leave the Ecomuseum, turn left onto Chemin Ste-Marie, and continue east until Boulevard Morgan. Follow signs for Highway 40 Est.

Shopping

Though *Québécois* fight for French, they consume American, so visitors often discover the best buys in Montréal before the locals. Boutiques show sleek Continental styles, antique dealers proffer frontier pine and Old World heirlooms. Shops display rafts *fait à main* (handmade) by Inuit, Amerindian, or other local artists. Place Bonaventure regularly hosts major shows: books in November, antiques and crafts in December.

Shopping ranges from functional underground mazes of mainstream and chain stores, packed in winter, to sumptuous arcades filled with light and art. You can follow banners to *la Cité de la mode* or *le district de la fourrure* for stylish clothing, including leather, and furs, that make Montréal a trendsetter.

Wherever you go, look for deals. Though the black market isn't strong anymore, the recession still causes prices to fluctuate. As a visitor, you can reclaim some tax *(see Practical Information, page 73)*. Although shopping hours vary with locale and season, the following is typical: 9 or 10am–6pm most weekdays, to 9pm Thursday, Friday, and holidays. Sunday shopping, still relatively new to Quebec, has gained popularity, though some hours may be restricted.

With the metro as its spine, Montréal's downtown fosters an elaborate *réseau souterrain,* massive underground mall. What began

All-weather shopping

as a simple shopping center beneath the city's first high-rise at Place Ville Marie in 1962 has blossomed to an underground labyrinth of walkways stretching 29 km (18 miles) with 1,700 shops, two department stores, 200 restaurants, 34 cinemas and theaters, plus murals, plaques, and basement musicians.

The advantages of this underground city are that it is comfortable, efficient, safe, and relatively clean, and provides protection from the bitter winter temperatures. If you get lost, don't worry. Most out-of-towners need help through the maze, and locals will literally take you by the hand. Ticket-takers at metro booths will also dish out maps and precise directions. Also,

come up for light and air periodically, as the artificial lighting and the constant 22°C (72°F) temperature can be disorienting.

Montréal also has shopping malls that start underground and spiral upwards. You usually enter by escalators in commercial complexes. But beware, rocky economic times have closed many shops, so some centers may be disturbingly quiet. But often the setting is so spectacular that it's worth a visit. Try **Les Cours Mont-Royal**, at 1455 Peel, where a winding staircase links three levels in the exquisite lobby of the former Hotel Mont-Royal. Here's true splendor: a grand entrance and stunning chandelier. **Place Montréal Trust**, at McGill College and Ste-Catherine, offers 120 shops, with sunlight filtering through atrium corridors and a fountain cascading from the fifth floor. **Les Promenades de la Cathédrale**, directly below Christ Church Cathedral, at 625 Ste-Catherine Ouest, has 100 shops on two levels.

Also note Montréal's fine downtown **department stores**. Two of the best are **Ogilvy**, at 1307 Ste-Catherine Ouest, and **Holt Renfrew**, 1300 Sherbrooke Ouest – both landmarks of good taste. **La Baie**, founded as the Hudson Bay Company in 1670, offers tradition at 585 Ste-Catherine Ouest. For high style and prices to match, look to the area between Mount Royal, Westmount and Outremont. At **Westmount Square**, architect Mies van der Rohe's elegant office complex has equally elegant shops tucked underneath. Ready-to-wear and designer labels come in pretty packages. Above ground, head to **Avenue Greene**. Its Main Street is a mix of boutiques and local stores.

Between Rue Querbes in Outremont and Boulevard St-Laurent in Montréal, **Rue Laurier Ouest** offers style (home furnishings, maternity, children's) for affluent francophones. The names are international, but weighted towards French, with a nod to kilts and crests. Besides *haute couture*, there's *haute cuisine*. Indulge at any of the many gourmet food purveyors on Laurier for the take-out pleasures of French cooking.

Antiques

Laid out in the 1660s, **Rue Notre-Dame** once served as the *Chemin du Roi* – the King's Highway to Quebec City. Today, many of its graystones house Montréal's best antique shops. You will fine a clump of them immediately east of Lionel-Groux metro, scattered along both north and south sides of Notre-Dame. The bulk of them, about a dozen shops, are found further east, on the south side of Notre-Dame, between Canning and Guy. A useful tip: bargaining with cash will invariably ease a deal.

Headpiece

Bagging bargains at the sales

Handicrafts

The amount of *camelote* (junk) in the typical souvenir shop can be depressing. Only a handful of shops offer some relief, with their impressive ranges of quality provincial crafts. The dowager among these is the **Canadian Guild of Crafts**, 2025 Peel. Dating from 1905, this non-profit-making organization has over 200 members – crafts workers and patrons who support the gallery in a renovated mansion downtown. Inuit, Amerindian and contemporary crafts are on sale. Don't miss the Inuit crafts tucked away upstairs – they're not for sale, but snooping is definitely recommended. Also look for quality service and crafts at **L'Impreinte Coopérative**, 272 St-Paul Est, in Old Montréal.

Fur and Clothes

Here in cold-clime Quebec, you'll find serious winter wear: practical, fashionable, furry, and sporty. At least five Quebec designers work 'distinctively Canadian' fashion into fur. Look out for dyed-to-shock color, native designs appliquéed with beads, and stenciling in offbeat patterns. High-class patchwork of recycled and unmatched fur is also very popular.

Visit the fur district for quality, reliability and, since fur's fashion rennaissance, style. Local designers to look out for are Zuki Bailala, who uses outrageous colors, and D'Arcy Moses and Ingrid Klahn who rely on a mixture of aboriginal and nature-inspired designs *(see Pick & Mix, Itinerary 1, page 38 for further details)*.

For ready-to-wear, try **Azimut Plein Air**, 1781 St-Denis, and **Kanuk**, 485 Rachel Est. For the best selection of local designers, look for **Revenge** at 3852 St-Denis and **Scandale**, 3639 St-Laurent.

Fancy a fur?

Eating Out

Ignoring food in Montréal is like ignoring snow in winter. You can't – you're surrounded. This is a city that teems with places to eat and drink: bars, bistros, brasseries, cafés, delis, pubs, restaurants, even festivals celebrating fondue, lobsters, and mussels. Here, even a *casse croûte* can taste great.

The city's long tradition of fine food dates from the 19th century, when Montréalers welcomed boats carrying tea from China, spices from India, and wines and spirits from Europe. But variety comes from France, famed for its food, and from immigrants, who began arriving here in the early 1900s and are still arriving, woks and *paella* pans in hand. Although the ethnic mix has occasionally created tensions on other fronts, Montréalers embraced new cuisines enthusiastically. So much so, that sometimes visitors have trouble finding restaurants that serve traditional *Québécois* cooking.

Where to feast? Check out likely restaurants that you have passed during the day. By law, eateries must post their menus outside or in the window, and most are bilingual. Consider the *table d'hôte* (set menu) to focus your choice and protect your

Wining and dining

pocketbook, though even *à la carte* meals are reasonably priced. Because you won't find *chien chauds* (hot dogs) sold on the street, lunch may be just a quick stop at the corner café. However, dinner in Montréal should be an event, carefully chosen, taking many hours and involving many different courses, all lovingly prepared and lovingly eaten.

Montréal offers a choice of some 4,000 restaurants, reportedly more per capita than anywhere else. Because residents consider themselves *connoisseurs* not only of food, but of service and setting, only exceptional restaurants survive. Even without trying, you'll find what locals call *honnête* (honest), good-value food, fresh and filling, if not imaginative.

Still confused? If you really can't decide where or what to eat, ask anyone – from the hotel maid to the newspaper vendor.

A few practical tips before feasting: some restaurants have no bar licences, and so can only serve alcohol with food. Some have bar permits and can serve drinks without food. Others with no permits allow guests to bring wine. Buy wine in a Société des Alcools liquor store run by the province. They're cheaper and better stocked than the local *dépanneur* (convenience store).

Tax in restaurants is 15.56 percent, and a tip is 10–15 percent of the pre-tax bill. Bar bills include tax, with 10 percent tips customary. In the following list, $ = under $15, $$ = $15–25, $$$ = $25–35, $$$$ = $35-plus (per person, excluding tax, tip and wine).

Specialties (all of these are $)

The most notable specialty is **smoked meat**. The city's Jewish population has fostered unresolved debates over where to find 'the best'. Here's how: eat your way through **Schwartz** and **The Main** on St-Laurent, then head to **Ben's**, 990 de Maisonneuve Ouest (tel: 844-1000), with its pictures of stage and screen greats. Or join lunch-time line-ups at **Wilensky**, 34 Fairmount Ouest (tel: 271-0247), where you can settle for beef, fried baloney, or salami with mustard on a toasted bun.

In this city, **bagels** are made 'the old way', with honeyed water for sweetness and wood fires for heat and flavor. For eight varieties, go to **Fairmount Bagel Bakery**, 74 Fairmount Ouest (tel: 272-0667), or try **St-Viateur Bagel**, nearby at 158 and 263 St-Viateur Ouest, specializing in white sesame and black poppyseed. Standing next to you in line may be neighborhood Hassidim men wearing long black coats and fur-trimmed hats and women dressed modestly in 18th-century Eastern European styles.

For special fast food and drink, consider ubiquitous **St-Hubert Bar BQ** for chicken, **Pizzedelic** or **Pizzaiolle** for you-ate-it-here-first combos, or any of 30 **La Cage Aux Sports** outlets for giant-screen meals.

Smoked meat: a specialty

Track down **Les Fleurs** for steamies and *patates frites*. At the **Orange Julep**, 7700 Décarie Est (tel: 738-7486), an orange-colored-and-shaped hut dispenses refreshing orange slurpies. **La Cervoise**, 4457 St-Laurent (tel: 843-6586), and **Le Cheval Blanc**, 809 Ontario Est (tel: 522-0211), serve beer brewed on the premises, with hard-to-come-by ales. Montréal is serious *café au lait* territory and St-Denis Street is littered with excellent coffee houses that you shouldn't miss.

Go to Ben's for smoked meat

Breakfast

BEAUTY'S RESTAURANT
93 Mont-Royal Ouest
Tel: 849-8883
Fixed menu served amid 1950s diner decor: fresh orange juice, bagels, mishmash (omelet with everything). $

CAFE TITANIC
445 St-Pierre
Tel: 849-0894
Bright and cheerful ambience. Also good for lunch. $

DUSTY'S RESTAURANT
4510 du Parc
Tel: 276-8525
Downscale, but all-day brunch with a choice of 23 types of omelets. $

LA VIEILLE FRANCE
52 St-Jacques

Bumper harvest

Tel: 845-1575
Classical music and singing accompany Sunday brunch. 'Repas chaud' buffet includes *terrine* pork and caribou. $$$

Hamburgers

L'ANECDOTE
801 Rachel Est
Tel: 526-7967
Serving the finest gourmet hamburgers, with milkshakes. $

LA PARYSE
302 Ontario Est
Tel: 842-2040
Popular student hangout. $

Steak and Seafood

LE BIFTHEQUE
6705 Côte-de-Liesse
Ville St-Laurent
Tel: 739-6336
A la carte at the largest steakhouse in town; pâtisserie and butcher shop. $$

CHEZ DELMO
211 Notre-Dame Ouest
Tel: 849-4061
Classic seafood and fish dishes. $$

CHEZ MAGNAN
2602 St-Patrick
Tel: 935-9647
A steakhouse with working-class ambience and quality steaks. $$

MOISHE'S
3961 St-Laurent
Tel: 845-3509
Old fashioned steak restaurant. Dress code. $$$

MILOS
5357 du Parc
Tel: 272-3522
Greek taverna with fresh fish. $$$$

Québécois

AUBERGE LE VIEUX ST-GABRIEL
426 St-Gabriel
Tel: 878-3561
North America's oldest inn (1754) serves *Québécois* cuisine. $$$

LA FESTIN DU GOUVERNEUR
The Old Fort, Ile Ste-Hélène
Tel: 879-1141
Re-enactment of a 17th-century banquet. $$$

TY-BREIZ CREPERIE BRETONNE
933 Rachel Est
Tel: 521-1444
Dinner and dessert crepes served in a smoky, down-to-earth, convivial little eatery. Extremely popular with French-speaking locals. $$$

Whetting the appetite

French

THE BEAVER CLUB
Hotel Reine Elizabeth
900 René Lévesque
Tel: 861-3511
Classic French cuisine served amid animal pelts and trophies. $$$$

CHEZ LA MERE MICHEL
1209 Rue Guy
Tel: 934-0473
Delectable and innovative French food; good wine selection. $$$$

LE P'TIT PLATEAU
330 Marie-Anne Est
Tel: 282-6342

Good bistro meals and plenty of French conversation and wine. $$$$

RESTAURANT LES HALLES
1450 Crescent
Tel: 844-2328
Gastronomic *tour de force*. $$$$

Vegetarian

CAFÉ SANTROPOL
3990 St-Urbain
Tel: 842-3110
Fruit spritzers, salads, huge sandwiches (and meat, too). Garden. $$

CHUCHAI
4088 St-Denis
Tel: 843-4194
Serves meat substitutes made from soy, wheat and seitan, with a take-away. $$

LE COMMENSAL
1204 Avenue McGill College
Tel: 871-1480
3715 Chemin Queen Mary
Tel: 733-9755
1720 St-Denis
Tel: 845-2627
Buffet with large salads, hot veggie meals and great desserts. $$

Oriental

CHAO PHRAYA
50 Laurier Ouest, tel: 272-5339
4088 St-Denis, tel: 843-4194
Excellent Thai food, with dishes spiced to taste. Reservations. $$

HONG KONG HOUSE
1023 St-Laurent
Tel: 861-0251
Try anything here. With 200 Chinese dishes, you're spoiled for choice. $$

JARDIN DE JADE-POON KAI
67 de la Gauchetière Ouest
Tel: 866-3127
All-you-can-eat Cantonese and Szechuan buffet. $

KATSURA
2170 de la Montagne
Tel: 849-1172
Sushi, teriyaki and *sashimi* platters tempt in *tatami* room. $$

MIYAKO
1439 Amherst
Tel: 521-5329
Good Japanese sushi bar. $$

THAI GRILL
5101 St-Laurant
Tel: 270-5566
Great Thai meals and lunchtime buffets; a locals' favorite. $$–$$$

ZEN
1050 Sherbrooke Ouest
Tel: 499-0801
Top restaurant with top prices, inside the Omni Hotel Mont-Royal. $$$

European

L'ACTUEL
1194 Peel
Tel: 866-1537
Popular restaurant serving mussels prepared in 13 different ways. $$

ARAHOVA
256 St-Viateur Ouest
Tel: 274-7828
Exceptional (and good value) *souvlaki* and other Greek specialties. $

Sweet sensations

BUONA NOTTE
3518 St-Laurent
Tel: 848-0644
Quality *nouvelle* Italian cuisine. $$

FONDUEMENTALE
4325 St-Denis
Tel: 499-1446
Feast on a choice of thirty different fondues from traditional cheese or chocolate to gorgonzola, goat cheese, or honey chicken. $$

IL MULINO
236 St-Zotique Est
Tel: 273-5776
This is another good option for authentic Italian. Limited number of dishes which change daily. $$$

MILOS
5357 du Parc
Tel: 272-3522
The city's top Greek restaurant, serving plenty of lamb, seafood and vine leaves. $$$$

STASH CAFE BAZAAR
200 St-Paul Ouest
Tel: 845-6611
Polish *borscht*, and dumplings. $$

JEAN TALON MARKET
Opened in 1933, the Jean Talon Market forms the heart of Montréal's 'Little Italy.' Here, more than 120 stall holders sell fresh fruits, vegetables and other produce. Cheese counters, butchers' stalls, fish stalls, and a variety of restaurants surround the main marketplace which is open Monday to Wednesday, 7am–6pm; Thursday to Friday 7am–9pm; weekends to 5pm. $

LE WITLOOF
3619 St-Denis
Tel: 281-0100
Popular late 19th-century bistro specializing in hearty Belgian cuisine. $$

Nightlife

Montréal's nightlife is wild and varied. An evening out often begins with drinks between 5 and 7pm and ends eight or nine hours later with a bleary-eyed breakfast in an all-night café. Montréal is certainly not the conservative Catholic place it was a few generations ago. Clubs and discos stay open until 3am, later than anywhere else in Canada, and sex shops and strip joints now generate more revenue than controversy. In nightclubs, style dominates the scene.

Nightlife is not relegated to the weekend. On Tuesday, Wednesday and Thursday, crowds gather in the Place-des-Arts cultural center, teens gyrate to rave and rock music, and film fanatics head for *le cinéma* or *les vues*.

Where to party? Almost anywhere. Bars, discos, and restaurants cluster downtown, along Ste-Catherine. The chic flock to *bôites de nuit* on St-Denis. Allophone St-Laurent hops to what's hip.

There is plenty of highbrow nightlife too. Montréal's symphony and opera earn ovations worldwide. Theaters offer experimental and traditional plays in French, English or both. Dance ranges from ballet and ballroom, to funk, techno, tropical, even oompah. Jazz drifts into blues. The Molson Centre rocks with big international names.

Try shaking it with the pretty things in a dance club or relaxing to jazz in a night club. Here's where and how:

Montréal lights up

Information and Tickets

Check local newspapers, especially Friday or weekend editions, and alternative papers. Call ahead for movies and plays where language may be an important factor; ask about cover charges.

For information on cultural events, call Tourisme Montréal on 844-5400, Monday to Saturday 11am–8pm, Sunday noon–5pm visit www.tourisme-montreal.org. To reserve tickets, call Admission Ticket Network: 790-1245 or 1 800-361-4595 toll free from Canada and the US. For more limited ticketing, try Tel-Spec: 790-2222.

Performing Arts

PLACE-DES-ARTS
175 Ste-Catherine Ouest
Tel: 842-2112
Place-des-Arts is Canada's major center for performing and visual arts. Opened in 1963, the complex houses five performance halls, including the 3,000-seat Salle Wilfrid Pelletier.

It is home for L'Orchestre Symphonique de Montréal (tel: 842-9951, tickets $18–$58), L'Opéra de Montréal (tel: 985-2222, tickets $38–$105), and Les Grands Ballets Canadiens (tel: 849-0269, tickets, $25–$56).

When performances are not sold out, same-day seats, or next, may be discounted, depending on availability. Reserve after 3.30pm and pay at 7pm at the box office. At Salle Wilfrid Pelletier, try for rows C to H in the orchestra or for front rows of first and second balconies.

Live Venues

LE SPECTRUM
318 Ste-Catherine Ouest
Tel: 861-5851
With dynamic acoustics, this former theater hosts headliners as well as local favorites. There are no reservations;

Music man

tickets are sold on a first come, first served basis only.

THEATRE ST-DENIS
1594 St-Denis
Tel: 849-4211
The fare is French in the largest hall (2,200 seats) after Place-des-Arts: concerts, comedy, plays, and major festivals. Try for front-row balcony, or orchestra fifth or sixth row.

CLUB SODA
1225 St-Laurent
Tel: 286-1010
Live bands plus comedy in French. This is one of the hippest spots in town, so make sure you dress up for the occasion.

LE PUB PEEL
1107 Ste-Catherine Ouest
Tel: 844-6769
With live music, cheap beer and cheap food – this is the perfect lure for college crowds.

METROPOLIS
59 Ste-Catherine Est
Tel: 844-3500
Mega-disco, offering state-of-the art sound and light.

THE MOLSON CENTRE
1250 La Gauchetière Ouest
Tel: 932-2582
Major entertainments and business events venue, offering hockey games,

concerts, art and family shows. Includes a multi-functional amphitheater.

Theater

Some theaters –Théâtre de Quat'Sous, Théâtre d'Aujourd'hui – offer plays in French only from September to May. Others are year-round.

THEATRE DU RIDEAU VERT
4664 St-Denis
Tel: 844-1793
Classical repertory and contemporary theater performed in French.

CENTAUR THEATRE
453 St-Francois Xavier
Tel: 288-1229
Montréal's best-known English-language theater provides varied plays, good design, fine acoustics located in the Old Stock Exchange building.

SAIDYE BRONFMAN CENTRE
5170 Chemin de la Côte
Ste-Catherine
Tel: 739-2301
This 300-seat theater offers a range of plays, dance, music and special programs for children in both English and Yiddish.

L'ECOLE DE THEATRE/
NATIONAL THEATRE SCHOOL
1822 St-Laurent
Tel: 842-7954
The school offers four English and four French shows each year, with tickets available from the National Monument box office.

NOUVEAU COMPAGNIE THEATRALE
NCT
4353 Ste-Catherine Est
Tel: 253-8974
Salle Denise Pelletier and Salle Fred Barry stage a mix of plays, from the well-known to experimental and unilingual to bilingual.

Night Clubs

L'AIR DU TEMPS
191 St-Paul Ouest
Tel: 842-2003
Charming and comfortable bar offering top-quality jazz performances.

BIDDLES
2060 Aylmer
Tel: 842-8656
The home of jazzman Charlie Biddles, this place manages to combine classy with cozy. The food is especially good here – try the ribs and potatoes with skins.

LES FOUFOUNES ELECTRIQUES
87 Ste-Catherine Est
Tel: 844-5539
Attracting a mainly anti-conformist crowd, aged 16 plus, for grunge, hip hop, techno and metal, with decor like a futuristic movie-set. Huge space, cheap prices, long lines. Check out the terrace.

PASSEPORT
4156 St-Denis
Tel: 842-6063
This favorite Plateau nightspot is concealed by a shop during daylight hours. By night, the venue transforms into a haven of soul.

LE QUAI DES BRUMES
4481 St-Denis
Tel: 499-0467
This brasserie mixes blues and rock in a beer-hall muted by paneled wood and Tiffany lighting.

Cinema

LA CINEMATHEQUE QUEBECOISE
335 de Maisonneuve Est
Tel: 842-9763
Quebec, Canadian, foreign, classic, retrospectives, animated and silent films.

ONF/NATIONAL FILM BOARD
1564 St-Denis
Tel: ONF-FILM or NFB-FILM.
Canada's major filmmakers fill the screens. Also video and laser disk.

IMAX
Old Port
Tel: 496-IMAX
Gripping visuals projected on seven-story screens include 3-D and high-definition exclusives, all larger-than-life and year-round.

THE IMPERIAL
1432 Bleury
Tel: 848-0300
Excellent sounds and wide seats, in a restored movie palace, make this first-run cinema worth the money.

LE RIALTO
5723 du Parc
Tel: 272-3899
This *grande dame* offers live theater, music, and first-run independent films.

Dance

ACADEMIE DE TANGO
4445 St-Laurent
Tel: 840-9246
Strap on your dance shoes. Tango on Friday and Saturday nights, from 9.30pm–3am and Sundays at 8pm, to watch or join in.

ALLEGRA
3523A St-Laurent
Tel: 288-4883
Hops to live Latin American music on Thursday, world beat, R&B, funk and even swing on other nights.

LA SALSATHEQUE
1220 Peel
Tel: 875-0016
Salsa, with a large dose of mainstream disco tossed in.

Comedy, etc

CIRQUE DU SOLEIL
8400 2nd Avenue
Tel: 722-2324
A circus with no animals and only one ring? Yet Cirque du Soleil rivets its audiences with three hours of amazing acrobatic feats. Begun as ragtag street performers in Baie St-Paul in 1984, the troupe went on to achieve tremendous worldwide fame, but they always return to Montréal to launch new programs.

COMEDY NEST
4020 Ste-Catherine
Tel: 932-6378
An English showcase for local and out-of-town stand-up comics, this venue survives from its heyday in the 1970s. Also includes a restaurant.

Cirque du Soleil

Calendar of Special Events

Trapped indoors by winter, Montréalers claim back their city's streets for summer festivals. They grab every chance to gather: music, comedy, sports, film, partying frenetically and non-stop. Often, out-of-towners join the locals to turn downtown streets into human traffic jams as half a million people head out to be where jazz notes float above outdoor stages, where clowns and mimes tease belly laughs from crowds, and where fireworks send aficionados scrambling for the best vantage points.

Buy seats for ticketed events in indoor venues or create your own free seat on the street, even if it's only on a sidewalk curb. Street entertainment can be a dollar-watcher's delight, as much of it is free.

JANUARY / FEBRUARY

For 10 days each February, the **Snow Festival**/La Fête des Neiges takes the chill out of winter, filling Parc Jean-Drapeau with snow castles, giant ice slides, and ice sculptures. For action, look for, or join competitions in, kite skating, barrel-jumping, and dog sled or ice canoe racing. Mascot *Boule de Neige* leads the fun. (Tel: 872-4537.)

MAY / JUNE

As far as festivals are concerned March and April are quiet months, but Summer festivities get going around May. Throughout June and July, representatives from a dozen countries blast fireworks during eight consecutive weekends in the **International Fireworks Competition**. Shows begin after dusk, usually at 10pm at La Ronde amusement park on Ile Ste-Hélène. But the view is good, and free, from the city side, near Frontenac metro station or from the Jacques Cartier Bridge. Each spectacle lasts half an hour; the oohs and aahhs longer. (Tel: 872-4537.)

In mid-June, look for Canada's only world circuit of Formula One racing and the world's only circuit on an island: Ile Notre-Dame. More than 100,000 fans come to the three-day event at the **Air Canada Grand Prix**

Don't miss the International Fireworks Competition

Clowning around in summer

on the 4.4-km (2¾-mile) Gilles Villeneuve track. (Tel: 350-0000.)

One day each June, as many as 45,000 cyclists pedal a 65-km (40-mile) route in **Le Tour de l'Ile de Montréal**. The route varies, sometimes inside city limits, sometimes out. Join the Express Tour that leaves ahead of the crowd, averaging 35 km/h (22 mph). The Bistro du Tour hosts entertainers near the finish line. (Tel: 521-8687.) At the end of June, the **Carifête** festival is a chance to celebrate the city's Caribbean community.

JULY / AUGUST

Early to mid-July, jazz and blues performers converge here from all over the world for 10 or more days with 300 concerts at the **International Jazz Festival**/Festival International de Jazz de Montréal. Big-name performers take over large venues and local clubs for ticketed concerts, but others are held outdoors and are free, day and night. Good music in 350 shows lures more than a million visitors. (Tel: 523-3378)

For 10 days from mid-July to early August, the city hosts the **Just for Laughs Festival**/Festival Juste Pour Rire. In one of the world's premier comedy festivals, nearly 500 performers from more than a dozen countries stage 300 shows, indoors and out, making this the world's largest bilingual comedy routine. You will find acrobats, street comedians, stage comedians, mime artists, and clowns. (Tel: 845-3155.) In late July, **Nuits d'Afrique** celebrates African culture and cuisine with street music, dance and traditional foods.

Artists world-wide offer French songs and skits at **Les Francofolies de Montréal**, for 10 days in early August. Expect anything from African music to French rap or even Quebec folk songs. (Tel: 876-8989.)

The **International Festival of Gastronomy**/Les Fêtes Gourmandes Internationales first celebrated the city's 350th birthday in 1992. Mid-August, restaurants offer outdoor feasts on Ile Notre-Dame. Try Quebec wild boar, Vietnamese spring rolls, or Italian *spumone* (ice-cream). (Tel: 861-8241.)

From late August to early September, film-makers and film-goers go into overdrive for 10 days at the **Montréal World Film Festival**/Festival des Films du Monde. Film producers rank this festival 'category A,' up there with Cannes and Venice. (Tel: 848-3883.)

SEPTEMBER / OCTOBER

For three weeks in mid-September, each odd-numbered year, the **International Festival of New Dance**/Festival International de Nouvelle Danse features dancers and choreographers from around the world. (Tel: 287-1423.)

NOVEMBER / DECEMBER

Celebrations die down as Montréalers begin their winter hibernation. Festivities revive at Christmas.

Practical Information

TRAVEL ESSENTIALS

Visas / Passports / Customs

Everyone entering Canada from any country but the United States must have a valid passport, and may require a visa. US citizens or permanent residents need only identity papers: driver's license plus birth certificate. Visitors staying longer than three months may need a visa. Border formalities are usually simple and fast – so long as you leave handguns or automatic weapons at home. For further details contact: Ministère des Affaires Extérieures du Canada. Tel: 283-2152, 1-800-267-8376 (toll free); www.dfait-maeci.gc.ca.

Consulates

If you need to reach your government, consult the *Yellow Pages*. More than 50 countries have consulates in Montréal, including: France (tel: 878-4381), the US (tel: 398-9695), and the United Kingdom (tel: 866-5863).

Arrival

By air: Two Montréal airports handle international flights: **Dorval**, for domestic and US flights and **Mirabel**, for all other international flights (tel for both airports: 394-7377). Dorval, which is small, outdated and busy, is about 22 km (14 miles), half-an-hour's drive, from downtown Montréal. Mirabel, which is vast, modern and underused, is about 55 km (34 miles), or 45 minutes from downtown Montréal. Taxis set fares by flat rate or zone.

It's 47 km (29 miles), or 35 minutes between airports. A taxi between Mirabel and Dorval costs about $60, between Mirabel and downtown Montréal about $65, between Dorval and downtown Montréal about $30. Limousines can cost double this.

An airport bus travels between Mirabel and the Voyageur bus terminal at downtown Central Station and the new city-center air terminal at la Gauchetière and University, (tel: 394-7369). A regular bus also serves Dorval. Check counters on the air terminal's ground floor. Both are operated by Aerobus (tel: 399-9877).

By Bus: The bus station for all long distance routes is the Voyageur Terminal (Berri-UQAM Metro station), 505 de Maisonneuve Est (tel: 842-2281).

By Train: Amtrak (tel: 1-800-872-7245) and VIA Rail (tel: 989-2626; www.viarail.ca). Trains arrive downtown at Central Station (Bonaventure metro station), 935 de la Gauchetière Ouest. Bonaventure metro links both regional and commuter trains.

By Road: Canada's premier highway, the Trans Canada, forks on reaching Montréal, with autoroute 40 (Boulevard Métropolitain) crossing the city's northern neighborhoods east to west, and autoroute

Flying the flag

20 (Autoroute Ville Marie) traveling along the south shore of the St Lawrence, over the Jacques Cartier Bridge into the city and along its southern edge.

Both routes are poorly designed and maintained, with twists and narrow ramps. Speed limits are 50 km/h (30 mph) in cities, 80 km/h (50 mph) on two-lane highways, and 100 km/h (62 mph) on freeways. Safety belts must be worn.

Two of Montréal's 1.1 million

GETTING ACQUAINTED
Population / Geography

Montréal is a bustling city and island, at the confluence of the Ottawa river and St Lawrence Seaway that leads northeast to the Atlantic Ocean and southwest to the Great Lakes. Lengthwise, tip to tip, the island stretches 50 km (32 miles) and widens to 16 km (10 miles).

The city has a population of 1.1 million, with another 2.1 million in 'greater Montréal.' After Toronto, it's Canada's largest city. Located in Québec province, Montréal is 72 km (45 miles) north of the US border, in the center of the St Lawrence lowlands – flanked by the Canadian shield to the north, Appalachians to the south and east, and Adirondacks to the south.

The curve in Montréal's croissant shape confounds directions, with designated northern and southern areas often really east and west. Sherbrooke, the east-west axis, runs north-south at times. With that in mind, on north-south streets building numbers increase as you head north, with even ones on the west, or left. Boulevard St-Laurent divides the city east and west.

Language

Montréalers speak, work and sing in French, and expect everyone else to do the same. Francophone *Québécois* take their language seriously, at times backing laws and litigation in support of it.

Elsewhere in Canada, the two languages of the 'founding nations' are official. But here provincial law mandates that only French is the official language for business and government. Grammar lapses, such as dropped apostrophes or a misplaced accent can be interpreted as political snubs. The battles swirl around the two groups, though allophones who speak neither French nor English as their first language are gaining impact. Usually squabbles focus on signs in English that are not subordinate to French. Only rarely do third languages – say, Chinese – draw ire.

Because most language issues are political rather than personal, such local squabbles shouldn't discourage visitors. Even if you don't speak much French, starting a conversation with '*Bonjour*,' is likely to evoke a positive response. Indeed, some shopkeepers hedge with an all-purpose: 'Hi-*bonjour.*'

Montréal claims to be the second-largest French-speaking city in the world, after Paris. Some 65 percent of the city's residents and 70 percent of those in the metropolitan area are French-speakers (francophones), with 12 percent and 15 percent English-speakers (anglophones), respectively. Despite nationalistic insistence, the province's French has never been pure. After 300 years of separation from the motherland, how could it be? French speakers will encounter many unfamiliar turns of phrase. Over the past decades, as Montréalers have acknowledged differences and gained confidence, this has become amusing rather than disconcerting.

71

Montréalers digging their way out of winter

Unique to Montréal is *joual*, a patois whose name is garbled French for horse: *cheval*. The earthy dialect flourishes among the city's working class and in the work of playwright Michel Tremblay.

Pronunciation of mainstream French also differs. Accents distinguish French in Quebec from French in Paris or Marseilles. Quebec's francophones form sounds deep in the throat, lisp slightly, voice toward diphthongs, and bend single vowels into exotic shapes. Many Montréalers are bilingual; some are trilingual. Immigrants have introduced wide linguistic diversity. There are residents from some 80 countries speaking, among them, an estimated 35 different languages.

Weights and Measures

Canada operates on the metric system of weights and measures. Temperature is given in degrees Celsius, gasoline sold by the liter, groceries weighed in grams and kilograms, and road speeds posted in kilometers per hour.

Time

Montréal follows Eastern Standard Time, adopting daylight savings time (clocks go forward one hour) in early April and reverting to standard time (back one hour) in late October.

Electricity

Electrical current is 110 volts, 60 cycles, alternating current. Appliances from the US do not need converters; those from Europe do.

Weather

If you want to find Montréalers in mid-winter, head south to Florida, for winters at home are harsh. Winter is technically mid-November to mid-April, but temperatures may dip below freezing in early November, and snow may hang on until May.

Mid-March usually signals spring, though April and May can be chilly and rainy. June, July and August are typically hot and humid. Between late September and mid-November, the weather gets progressively cooler. The sun can dazzle in summer or winter, so pack your sunglasses. Bring a sweater for summer evenings, and many sweaters and scarves for winter.

Temperatures veer drastically over the year, with temperatures in January averaging -9.5°C (15°F), and in July averaging 21°C (70 °F) and sometimes hitting 30°C (86°F). Overall winter temperatures average -8°C (18° F), so wrap up well if you arrive mid-winter. Rainfall averages 78 cm (31 in), with annual snowfall exceeding 242 cm (95 in). Luckily, the city has the world's best snow removers.

For weather information, call: Environment Canada, tel: 1-800-463-4311.

HEALTH AND EMERGENCY

Emergency Telephone Numbers
Police, fire, ambulance; tel: **911**

Doctors, dentists and opticians
Contact Information and Referral Center

of Greater Montréal (Monday to Friday 8.30am–4.45pm), tel: 527-1375. For dentists, contact Ordre des Dentistes du Québec, tel: 875-8511. For opticians, contact Ordre des Opticiens d'Ordonnances du Québec, tel: 288-7542. Most major hospitals with 24-hour emergency rooms have English-speaking staff.

Anti-poison Center, tel: 1-800-463-5060 (toll free).

24-hour Pharmacy
Pharmaprix
901 Ste-Catherine Est and
5122 Côte-des-Neiges
Tel: 738-8464

24-hour Emergency Treatment
Hôpital Hôtel-Dieu de Montréal
3840 St-Urbain
Tel: 843-2611

Hôpital St-Luc
1058 St-Denis
Tel: 890-8000

Hôpital Royal Victoria
687 Rue des Pins Ouest
Tel: 842-1231

Hôpital Général de Montréal
1650 Avenue du Cédar
Tel: 937-6011

24-hour Emergency Dentistry
The Dental Clinic
3546 Rue Van-Horne
Tel: 342-4444

MONEY MATTERS

Banking
Monday to Friday, 10am–4pm. Some branches offer Saturday service.

Currency Exchanges
Currency can be exchanged at major banks and foreign exchange dealers (any amount). Rates at banks are generally better. The common bills – $5, $10, $20 – vary in color. The $1 coin is called a loonie; the $2 is a dubloonie. In tourist areas, other currencies, especially US dollars, are accepted, though not at the best rate.

Tipping
Coat checkers, doormen, and porters normally expect around $1 per item. Waiting staff and taxi drivers expect 10–15 percent of the bill or fare. Some restaurants may add an automatic service charge for groups. Word of warning: be careful not to tip on the bill's combined provincial (PST)/federal (GST) sales tax, which adds 15.6 percent to the total.

Tax relief
A 7 percent federal tax (GST/TPS) is applied to most goods and services in Canada. In addition to this a Quebec provincial tax (PST/TVQ) is added to all goods (8 percent) and services (4 percent).

Visitors can apply for a GST rebate on short-term accommodations and most goods bought for use outside Canada. To do this you will need to apply for the form 'GST rebate for visitors,' which is available from *Revenue Canada's* Ottawa office and most tourist shops. A rebate of up to $500 can be claimed by mail or in person at duty-free shops at the borders and airports.

A palatial bank

Applications for GST rebates must include original bills of sale or itemized receipts. Accommodation receipts must show the number of nights of lodging supplied. For more details, tel: 847-0982 in Montréal, 1-800-668-4748 (toll free) or 920-432-5608 outside Canada.

Some merchants offer to pay the taxes, while other traders offer discounts for cash deals, which feed the underground economy and not the revenue collectors.

Telephone

Code for Canada: 1
Code for Montréal: 514
Information: 411
Assistance: 0
International access codes:
AT&T: 1-800-CALL ATT
MCI: 1-800-757-6655.
Sprint: 1-800-877-8000.

Postal Service

Post offices generally open from 8am–5pm, Monday to Friday, but closed Saturday. Canada Post, tel: 344-8822.

The central office at 1250 Université is full-service, including general delivery (tel: 395-4539). Stamps are available at coin machines in airports, terminals, and hotel lobbies.

Newspapers

Two free English-language tabloids, *The Mirror* and *Hour*, and their French-language counterparts, *Voir* and *Ici*, are published weekly. They list clubs, restaurants and entertainment beyond those covered by mainstream publications.

The Gazette is Montréal's only English daily. For French newspapers, choose *La Presse*, the city's largest daily; *Le Journal de Montréal*, a daily tabloid; *Le Devoir*, a daily for the province's intelligentsia, and *Allô Police*, a daily with lurid crime coverage for the not-so-intelligentsia.

HOURS AND HOLIDAYS

Business hours

Most businesses are open 9am–5pm. Museums follow regular business hours, but close either Monday or Tuesday. Shops are generally open Monday to Wednesday 10am–6pm, to 9pm on Thursday and Friday, and Saturday 10am–5pm. Many stores also open on Sunday.

Public holidays

New Year's Day January 1
Good Friday *varies*
Easter Monday *varies*
Dollard des Ormeaux Day (formerly Victoria Day): closest Monday to May 21
La Fête Nationale/St-Jean Baptiste Day: June 24
Canada Day: July 1
Labor Day: first Monday in September
Thanksgiving Day: second Monday in October
Remembrance Day: November 11
Christmas Day December 25
Boxing Day December 26

GETTING AROUND

Private cars

Driving in Montréal can be tricky. Speed limits and distances are posted in metric, but drivers dart about as if kph were mph (to convert kilometers to miles, multiply by 6 and divide by 10). Traffic signs are unilingual, French only. Some pictograms are highly developed; others, quite obscure.

It's controlled chaos on the streets. To survive, wear seatbelts – it's also the law. Contrary to other provinces, Quebec bans right turns on red lights. A flashing green arrow or light permits you to turn left while oncoming traffic is stopped. Though

Local number plate

pedestrians have the right of way at crosswalks, drivers ignore this. Bus drivers have the right of way, and they use it.

The city has two seasons: winter and road repair. For summer construction reports, call InfoRoute, tel: 526-4636; for winter weather conditions, call Environment Canada, tel: 1-800-463-4311.

If you bring your own car into Canada, you must bring with you a valid driver's license, your vehicle registration, and liability insurance (damage to someone else's property or person) for a minimum of $50,000.

Let me take your number

Rental Cars

There are branches at the airports, major hotels, and downtown. For long distances, it is worth considering renting your car cross-border in Burlington, VT, for an unlimited mileage deal. The following agencies have several locations, including at both airports.

Rental companies include: **Budget**, tel: 866-7675, 1-800-268-8900 (Canada); **Thrifty**, tel: 845-5954, 1-800-367-2277 (Intl); **Hertz**, tel: 842-8537, 1-800-654-3131 (Intl); **National**, tel: 878-2771, 1-800-387-4747 (Canada); **Discount**, tel: 286-1554, 1-800-263-2355. For further details, and rates and reservations, visit: www.carrentalsmontréal.com.

Parking

Most major offices, hotels, and shopping centers have underground parking lots. Private and public lots are also available. Parking signs are complex, and fines are steep, with the cost of towing even exceeding the cost of the penalty. Call 280-4636 during work hours (911 otherwise) if your car has been towed away. A crack corps of parking commandos, dubbed 'green onions' for the uniforms they wear, enforce these parking laws.

Emergency road service

Canadian Automobile Association, CAA-Quebec, tel: 861-7111 weekdays or visit: www.caaquebec.com for pre-journey information. Road service: 1-800-336-HELP.

Taxis

Taxis are plentiful, with rates fixed at approximately $3.50 to start, plus $1 for every kilometer – check for fare increases. There is no extra charge for luggage. Some vehicles are equipped to carry disabled passengers.
Taxi Veteran, tel: 273-6351; **Taxi Diamond**, tel: 273-6331; **Taxi La Salle**, tel: 277-2552; **Taxi Co-op**, tel: 725-9885.

Bicycle Rentals

Cycle Pop, tel: 526-2525.
Vélo Aventure Montréal, tel: 847-0666.

Public Transport

Montréal has an excellent metro *(see map below)* and bus service – clean, safe, efficient, comfortable and quiet. To plot your daily route, call AUTOBUS (tel: 288-6287). Telephone outside the rush hours for the best chance of getting through.

Fares are posted in all buses, ticket collection booths and metro stations, in

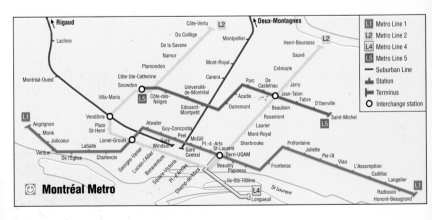

Montréal Metro

French and English. Board the bus with exact change or a ticket. Tickets are available in some stores, pharmacies, and all metro stations. One-day, three-day and monthly passes, and strips of six tickets are available at a discount.

Tickets are valid for bus and metro. Transfer tickets are valid in any direction for 90 minutes, between metro and bus, if you collect them on paying your fare.

More than 150 bus routes connect with 65 metro stations on four different lines, each distinguished by colors. Directions are indicated by end-of-the-line names. At night, the metro generally shuts down between 1 and 5.30am, although major bus routes continue through the night.

Designed by many architects, the stations are adorned with murals, sculptures and stained-glass windows. Older stations illustrate the city's history; newer stations feature abstract art.

Transit guides, pocket-sized maps of downtown, and commuter train schedules are available free at ticket booths. Bikes are permitted only outside rush hours.

By train: VIA Rail provides a service from coast to coast while Amtrak runs between Montréal and New York. Amtrak (tel: 871-9888) and VIA Rail (tel: 871-1331) trains arrive at Central Station, 1301 Bonaventure Place, near Bonaventure metro station. A Canrail pass allows discounts for VIA Rail travel on any 12 days in a 30-day period. Reserve early, especially between June and late-September, and holidays (tel: 1-800-361-5390). VIA Rail offers intercity, transcontinental, regional and remote services coast to coast.

By bus: The bus station for all long-distance bus routes is the Voyageur terminal, 505 de Maisonneuve Est, near Berri-UQAM metro station (tel: 842-2281). Voyageur bus offers 14-day unlimited travel fares from early May to late October, with extensions possible for a flat fee.

Taking a calèche

Follow the signs
Tours

Most tours focus on standard attractions, and guides are provided. Ask for senior discounts. Many of these tours depart from *Infotouriste*, 1001 Dorchester Square, tel: 873-2015, 1-800-363-7777 (toll free). Packages range from about $4–$60, half-day–full day, city only or beyond. Many run May through October only.

By bus
L'autre Montréal Tours, (non-profit in ethnic neighborhoods), tel: 521-7802.
Guidatour step-on service, tel: 844-4021.
Montréal Sightseeing, tel: 484-0104.
Murray Hill, tel: 331-9338.
Voyageur Bus Tours, tel: 842-2281.

By foot
Héritage Montréal funds walking tours focusing on architecture. Two-hour tours start at 2pm on summer weekends and are conducted in French and English. The charge is nominal. Tel: 286-2662.

By horse
Calèche rides go from Rue Notre-Dame, Mont-Royal, Place d'Armes and Place Jacques Cartier, tel: 496-7678. Especially popular during the winter months.

By boat
Bateau-mouche, tel: 849-9952.
Harbor Cruises, tel: 842-3871.
New Orleans Cruise, tel: 842-3871.
Lachine Rapids Tour, tel: 284-9607.
Amphitour, tel: 933-6674.

ACCOMMODATION

Montréal has more than 15,000 rooms to rent, some 23,000 in its metropolitan stretch. They range from luxurious for the rich to spartan for those on a budget. Besides familiar international chains, consider bed-and-breakfasts, college dorms, and campgrounds.

Prices peak during high season, May to October, but special rates and discounts may be available. In the past, occupancy rates have been as low as 55 percent, so ask around, as some hoteliers may be willing to negotiate room rates. The current daily average rate for a double room is around $100. Book in advance and always confirm rates.

Reservations

Réservation Québec offers no-cost research and reservations for 400 establishments in the province, tel: 1-800-363-7777.

Expensive ($100–250)

LE CHATEAU VERSAILLES
1659 Sherbrooke Ouest
Tel: 933-8111, 1-800-361-7199
(Canada), 1-800-361-3664 (US)
This hotel comprises four converted Edwardian stone townhouses and is close to every downtown site. If you prefer old elegance, avoid the modern tower.

LOEWS HOTEL VOGUE
1425 Rue de la Montagne
Tel: 285-5555
European luxury, with designer suites. It's well suited to business people and even has a fax in every room. It's worth paying a visit to this hotel even if you don't stay – the views are terrific.

L'INTER-CONTINENTAL MONTREAL
360 St-Antoine Ouest
Tel: 987-9900
Located at the World Trade Center, this landmark offers splendid, arched ceilings, plus bars, restaurants, adjoining shopping center and nearby convention center.

HOTEL OMNI MONT-ROYAL
1050 Sherbrooke Ouest
Tel: 284-1110, 1-800-268-6282 (toll free)

CAA 5-diamond rating. Spacious entrance, with health club attached.

RENAISSANCE MONTREAL
3625 du Parc
Tel: 288-6666, 1-800-363-0735 (toll free)
Central location with all amenities,

Le Château Versailles

including health club facilities. Linked to underground city.

RITZ-CARLTON MONTREAL
1228 Sherbrooke Ouest
Tel: 842-4212, 1-800-363-0366 (toll free)
The Ritz-Carlton Montréal has been a style-setter since the late 19th century. The location and service are unbeatable.

Moderate (under $100)

AUBERGE DE LA FONTAINE
1301 Rachel Est
Tel: 597-0166, 1-800-597-0597
Turreted graystone triplexes, some rooms with terraces or balconies. Breakfast, parking, kitchen. Office open 24 hours.

CROWNE PLAZA MONTREAL
506 Sherbrooke Est
Tel: 842-8581, 1-800-561-4644
Member of the world-wide chain, offering familiar basics.

DAYS INN DOWNTOWN MONTREAL
215 René Lévesque Est
Tel: 393-3388, 1-800-329-7416
Due to its location near to major convention centers and nightlife activity, this hotel is popular with business travelers.

HOTEL DE L'INSTITUT DU TOURISME ET D'HOTELLERIE DU QUEBEC
3535 St-Denis

B&B in a Victorian Mansion

Tel: 282-5120, 1-800-361-5111
What it lacks in charm, this institute makes up in value and service. A training ground for hotel and restaurant managers, the staff can be helpful. Student chefs prepare great meals at reasonable prices. Reserve early: only 42 rooms.

LES PASSANTS DU SANS SOUCY
171 St-Paul Ouest
Tel: 842-2634
Built in 1723, this 9-room hotel was once a fur warehouse. Now it's filled with brass beds and wooden furniture. Original beams and gables plus an art gallery.

Inexpensive (under $50)

AUBERGE DE JEUNESSE INTERNATIONAL/
INTERNATIONAL YOUTH HOSTEL
1030 MacKay
Tel: 843-3317
As well as 246 dormitory beds, there are private en-suite rooms. Communal kitchen.

MCGILL STUDENT APARTMENTS
3935 University
Tel: 398-6367
From mid-May to mid-August, spartan rooms in a grand location. Concordia University (848-4756) and Université de Montréal (343-6531) offer similar rooms in less central locations. Reserve July–August.

YMCA
1450 Stanley
Tel: 849-8393
Near Rue Sherbrooke. Most rooms available with shared facilities. Reserve for night or week, with varying rates.

YWCA
1355 René Lévesque Ouest
Tel: 866-9941
Reserve for night or week, with varying rates. Some rooms have semi-private baths.

Bed & Breakfasts

Perhaps more than anywhere else in North America, Montréal has embraced the European tradition of bed and breakfasts. Available homes – often restored Victorian mansions – tend to be centrally located in downtown, Westmount or Outremont. The following networks represent more than 50 homes in the city (more throughout the province). You receive an address when you reserve with a credit card. Prices vary according to room size, private bathroom, etc., but tend to range from $45–55 for a single, $65–90 for a double.

A Bed & Breakfast in Montréal, tel: 738-9410, 1-800-738-4338
Bed & Breakfast – A Downtown Network, tel: 289-9749
Hospitality Montréal Relais, tel: 287-9635/1-800-363-9635
Montréal Oasis in Downtown, tel: 935-2312

Camping

Camping Quebec classifies campgrounds according to quality of services and facilities. Participation is voluntary. For specifics, tel: 1-800-363-0457.
  Also contact the Association of Quebec Campgrounds, tel: 450-651-7396.

KOA-MONTREAL SOUTH
130 Monette Boulevard
Saint Philippe de la Prairie
Tel: 450-659-8626, 1-800-562-8636,
May 1 to October 10.

FURTHER INFORMATION
Tourist Offices

CENTRE INFOTOURISTE
1001 Square Dorchester
Guided bus tours, exchange offices, tourist information, travel agency, hotel bookings, bookstore, car rentals (open June 1 to Labor Day: daily 8.30am–7.30pm; Labor Day to May 31: 9am–6pm; tel: 873-2015 or 1-800-363-7777 (US and Canada).

Other locations offer more limited services and varied hours.

GREATER MONTRÉAL CONVENTION AND TOURISM BUREAU
1555 Rue Peel, bureau 600
Montréal, QC H3A 1X6.
Tel: 844-5400; fax: 844-5757;
www.tourism-montréal.org.

GOUVERNEMENT DU QUEBEC MINISTRE DU TOURISME
2 Place Québec, bureau 336
Quebec, G1R 2B5, tel: 418-528 8063;
www.gouv.qc.ca.

For other parts of Quebec, call Tourism Quebec, tel: 873-2015 or 1-800-363 7777 from elsewhere in North America. Or write to Tourisme Québec, Case postale 20000, Quebec, QC, G1K 7X2, Canada.

FURTHER READING

Insight Guide: Canada, APA Publications, 2001.

Insight Guide: Montréal, APA Publications, 2001.

Insight Guide: Vancouver, APA Publications, 1999.

Josh Freed, *Sign Language and Other Tales of Montréal Wildlife*, Montréal: Véhicule Press, 1990

Mordecai Richler, *Oh, Canada! Oh, Quebec! Requiem for a Divided Country*, Toronto: Penguin, 1992

Aline Gubbay, *A Street Called the Main*, Montréal: Meridian, 1989

Elaine Kalmna Nanes, *Writers of Montréal: Voix Parallèles/Parallel Voices*, Montréal: XYZ Editeur/Quarry, 1993

Barry Lazar and Tamsin Douglas, *Guide to Ethnic Montréal*, Montréal: Véhicule Press, 1993

BOOKSTORES

English

CAMELOT
1191 Place Phillips
Tel: 861-5019
The city's biggest and probably best computer software bookstore.

CHAPTERS
1171 Ste-Catherine Ouest
Tel: 849-8825
The city's largest English bookstore.

MCGILL UNIVERSITY BOOKSTORE
3420 McTavish
Tel: 398-7444
Strong on city and province.

French and English

ULYSSES
4176 St-Denis
Tel: 843-9447
Specialist in travel books, guides, maps.

French

LA CHAMPIGNY
4380 St-Denis
Tel: 844-2587
Continent's largest French-language bookstore, with over 100,000 titles.

GALLIMARD
3700 St-Laurent
Tel: 499-2012
Literary specialists with 65,000 titles.

Sunset over the Jacques Cartier Bridge

Index

NOTES